All God's Children

All God's Children

A Biblical Critique of Racism

Steven L. McKenzie

Westminster John Knox Press
Louisville, Kentucky

For information, address Westminster John Knox Press,
100 Witherspoon Street, Louisville, Kentucky 40202-1396

Quotations from the Bible, unless otherwise noted,
are the author's own translation.

Book design by Jennifer K. Cox
Cover design by Kevin Darst
Cover illustration courtesy of SuperStock

First edition
Published by Westminster John Knox Press
Louisville, Kentucky

This book is printed on acid-free paper that meets the
American National Standards Institute Z39.48 standard. ∞

PRINTED IN THE UNITED STATES OF AMERICA
98 99 00 01 02 03 04 05 06 — 10 9 8 7 6 5 4 3 2

Library of Congress Cataloging-in-Publication Data

McKenzie, Steven L., date.
    All God's children : a biblical critique of racism / Steven L.
McKenzie. — 1st ed.
        p.   cm.
    Includes bibliographical references.
    ISBN 0-664-25695-3 (alk. paper)
    1. Ethnology in the Bible.   2. Racism—Religious aspects—
Christianity.   3. Racism—Biblical teaching.   I. Title.
BS661.M44   1997
220.8'3058—dc21   96-45164

Contents

Preface

Racism in America

A photograph in *Newsweek* magazine the week the O.J. Simpson criminal trial ended (Oct. 16, 1995, pp. 26–27) said it all. It was a group of college students at the moment the verdict was announced. Every black face was jubilant; every white one, dumbfounded. The great legacy of that trial is that it brought home to white Americans the racial division that dominates our society. There had been signs of it in previous news items—the Rodney King beating and trial, for example. And the evidence of division is all around us. Jobs, neighborhoods, schools, and churches are divided too along racial lines. African Americans had long been aware that race profoundly affects this country's legal and civic institutions. O.J. vindicated their awareness by convincing white people that this is so.

Most white Americans have assumed that racism in the United States was essentially a thing of the past, that it had been legislated away, so that true to the civil rights song of the sixties, we had indeed overcome. Of course, they admitted there were isolated pockets where racism still existed. When I moved to Memphis in 1983, I immediately became aware that it contained more than its share of these pockets. But this was to be expected, since Memphis is in the South. The O.J. trial, however, exploded the myth that racism in America is confined to the South. And the truth is that his trial is only the most public example of the racism and racial division that exist nationwide.

Racism and the Bible

Race per se is a modern concept and therefore not an issue in the Bible. Nonetheless, the Bible has frequently been used in the past and continues to be used in the present to legitimate racist ideas and practices. Before and during the Civil War, Southern clergymen commonly cited the Bible not only in support of slavery but also to advocate black inferiority. The focal text for their sermons was Genesis 9, which is treated here in chapter 1. If this interpretation of the Bible had died with that generation, it would no longer matter. But as the story at the beginning of chapter 1 shows, this same interpretation continues to exercise a perverse influence today, over one hundred years later.

The continuing use of the Bible in defense of racism calls for a careful and reasoned analysis of its text. Such scholarly biblical analyses are available, but they tend to concentrate on technical matters of history, language, and composition and to ignore modern issues such as racism. This tendency is quite understandable, given the abuse to which the Bible is so often subjected in the service of all kinds of modern controversies. But my belief and contention in this book is that careful study of the Bible in context isolates a theological current that presents God's plan for humanity as a call for unity among all people and that, therefore, forcefully counters racism. There are, to be sure, examples of nationalism and ethnicism in the Bible that are the equivalent of racism. It is important to be honest in pointing these out and, without trying to minimize them, to understand them also in context. Nonetheless, there is a distinctive strain in the Bible as a whole that counters these narrow perspectives in a powerful way.

The Nature of This Book

The impulse for this book arose when Ken Sehested, director of the Baptist Peace Fellowship of North America, commissioned me to review a short pamphlet of reflections on racism and the Bible that the BPFNA was considering for publication. My critique confirmed Ken's suspicions that the reflections, while certainly well intentioned, contained serious historical and geographical errors. At the same time, the pamphlet and my conversations with Ken showed that there was clear, and indeed desperate, need for a detailed book on the topic.

This book will not, of course, make racism disappear. It is a complex social problem, one that is too ingrained in modern culture to be resolved by "throwing the Bible" at it. This book is intended, rather, as a resource to provoke thought and discussion about racism within religious communities. It not only counters claims that the Bible supports racism but also tries to show how important interracial unity is in the Bible's description of God's will for humanity. I hope that the case presented here will in turn lead readers to undertake concrete action to integrate and unify their communities.

Like any author, I write out of the limitations of my knowledge and experience, and I beg the reader to consider those limitations in evaluating this book. I am a white man who cannot pretend to share the perspectives of minorities or women. My approach is not "ideological critical," which would entail reading from a modern, deliberately ideological stance, such as that of an African American or a feminist critic. Rather, I attempt to interpret the biblical stories in their historical, cultural, and literary context as products of ancient Israel. It is my contention that from within that context the theology of the Bible speaks forcefully to the modern problem of racism. My area of expertise is the Hebrew Bible, so I hope my New Testament colleagues will pardon any treatments of materials in that area that remain facile, despite my efforts to consult experts. I am convinced of the value of interpreting the Hebrew Bible in its own context apart from later Christian use, and I believe the Hebrew Bible on its own makes some important theological statements relating to racism. At the same time, this book is designed specifically for a Christian lay audience, and I write from my Christian background. Hence, I ask the indulgence of my Jewish colleagues for using the term "Old Testament" throughout and for sometimes dealing with specifically Christian use and interpretation of Hebrew Scripture. Finally, the stories at the beginnings of each chapter relate specifically to the black civil rights movement in the United States. This is not meant to imply that other forms of racism do not exist in this country, that minorities other than African Americans have not been oppressed, or that racism is limited to the United States. It is simply that black-white racism is the most obvious and persistent and the civil rights movement the most current social upheaval against it. The biblical principles discussed in this book apply to racism in any form.

Acknowledgments

In addition to Ken Sehested, several individuals have served as "sounding boards" for the discussions in this volume, and I am grateful to each one of them. I thank Westminster John Knox Press, especially Jon Berquist, for seeing the potential of the idea and for their encouragement. My secretary, Karen Winterton, made the suggestion to include anecdotes at the beginning of each chapter to improve the book's readability and provide a springboard for sharing experiences within discussion groups. Along with personal experiences and stories I have heard about Memphis during my years here, the book *Voices of Freedom* was a wonderful source for stories from the civil rights movement.[1] Steve Haynes and Susan Sullivan, my colleagues at Rhodes College, have been my own discussion partners on this topic. Steve has been a constant source of information on the history of interpretation of the Bible, particularly of Genesis 9. Susan contributed, from her expertise, the sketch of Ida B. Wells's career at the beginning of chapter 4.

I owe a great deal to my family—especially in this case to my parents, who taught me early that racism is wrong. In this spirit, I dedicate this volume to two churches that in my experience have shown themselves dedicated to full racial integration and are making serious efforts toward that end: Riverside Church of Christ in Albuquerque, New Mexico, and Prescott Memorial Baptist Church in Memphis, Tennessee.

Steven L. McKenzie

Christmas 1995

part one

Beginnings

1

"In the Image of God"

Genesis 1—11

I shall never forget the session of a course I was teaching on the book of Genesis several years ago that treated the story from Genesis 9 on the so-called curse of Ham. This passage, or rather interpretations of it, provided the historical and theological basis among southern Christians prior to the Civil War for legitimating black slavery. At the time, I assumed that such interpretations were artifacts of the distant past. Most students were unfamiliar with them, so I first had to explain how the text had been used before I could show how such uses were misinterpretations. That day, though, the insidious tragedy of past misinterpretation was brought home to me. One of the students in the class, an African American, came up afterward to thank me. As a boy he had listened to his grandmother reading the Bible to him. He vividly recalled that when she came to this story she explained that black people were the descendants of Ham, who were cursed by the passage to be slaves to their white brothers. Their sufferings as a race, she said, were willed by God, a fated result of their being born black. This was not an understanding she had reached on her own but one she had been taught as the daughter of slaves by their white master. The student had inherited his grandmother's love for the Bible, but was disillusioned by a faith that affirmed the innate inferiority of an entire race—his race—as the will of God and that sanctioned their oppression. The class, he said, had restored his trust in the Bible as a source of comfort and inspiration rather than of oppression.

I have since become aware that the abuse of this passage for racial oppression is not nearly so defunct as I supposed it to be. The racist character played by Tom Berenger in the movie *Betrayed* (United Artists, 1988) realistically cites Genesis 9 in defense of his violent acts against blacks. I have heard a white supremacist preacher on television try to give this interpretation legitimacy by couching it in the guise of a reasoned explication of the text. I have even discovered a study Bible (*Dake's Annotated*), still being published in Georgia, that offers this racist explanation as the meaning of Genesis 9. It is in the hope of countering such interpretations that I offer the examination of Genesis 1—9 that comprises this chapter. The student whose story I have recounted is its inspiration.

Creation

Race is not an issue in the Bible in the way it is in modern society. The Bible's stories of creation do not distinguish different races as we might expect and as a creation story written today might do. This is particularly striking when one considers the nature of the Bible's creation accounts, especially the one in Genesis 2—3.

The first three chapters of the Bible are widely understood by scholars to contain two originally separate stories of creation. The distinction between the two is apparent in their respective orders of creation. Genesis 1 describes how God created the world in six days. It could almost be called a list, with a specific item or category of items being made on each day:

Day 1	—light
Day 2	—sky and seas
Day 3	—dry land and vegetation
Day 4	—sun, moon, and stars
Day 5	—birds and fish
Day 6	—land animals and people

The account extends into chapter 2, where the first three verses complete the first week by telling how God rested on the seventh day and thereby ordained the Sabbath as a day of rest and worship.

A new creation story begins in 2:4b and continues through chapter 3. Its nature and order are very different from those of the first chapter. It is, first of all, a narrative rather than a list.

It has characters (Yahweh[2] God, Adam, Eve, and the serpent), a plot, and character development. Its language and order are also quite different. In this story, Yahweh God first forms a man from the ground (2:7) and places him in the newly planted Garden of Eden (2:8), which stands alone in a world that is essentially a barren wasteland (2:5–6). Next, Yahweh God sets out to find a suitable companion for the man (2:18) and forms the animals out of the ground. But no animal is found to be "like him" or "corresponding to him" (2:18, 20). Taking one of the man's ribs (2:21) ensures that the new creature will be an appropriate match. With the rib Yahweh God "builds" a woman (2:22). The man's words upon seeing her make it clear that she is indeed like him: "This one, this time, is bone of my bone and flesh of my flesh" (Genesis 2:23). The order of the second creation story, therefore, is quite different from that of Genesis 1:1–2:3, and may be outlined as follows:

> a man
> a garden
> the animals
> a woman

Despite their obvious differences, these two accounts of creation have some common links, and the story in 2:4b–3:24 may have been interpreted by the editor who combined the two as a sequel or elaboration of the "list" in 1:1–2:3. One of the links between the two texts, which is important for the study of racism, is their use of the Hebrew word, 'adam. This word is often translated "man," and comparable to the older usage of that term in English 'adam can have at least five different meanings in Genesis 1—3, depending on the context:

1. all human beings, humankind (formerly "man" or "mankind")

2. an individual human, a person regardless of gender (German *man*)

3. all male humans, the male gender, "man" as opposed to "woman"

4. an individual male human, a man

5. the proper name "Adam"

Genesis 1:27 is an excellent example of the first meaning:

> So God created 'adam in his image; in the image of God
> he created them [Hebrew "him"]; male and female he cre-
> ated them.

The word 'adam here is defined as including male and female,
so that it refers to humans or humankind in general. Before its
combination with the story in chapters 2—3, this version of
creation did not presuppose that 1:27 referred to Adam and
Eve. Rather, Genesis 1:27 meant that God created all the people on earth (hundreds? thousands? of men and women) at one
time.

In 2:7, however, 'adam has a different meaning. This 'adam
is clearly an individual rather than the entire species. On the
other hand, since he is the only one of his species at this point,
he also represents all humans. He is, therefore, a *symbol* of humankind. He is also probably a representative or symbol of all
males or men (definition 3). There is some debate as to whether
'adam at this stage should be understood as genderless, or
rather androgynous (i.e., combining both genders), or as a
male. But v. 23 clarifies this matter when it says that the
woman was taken from (or "out of") the man, using a word for
"man" that is gender-specific (Hebrew 'ish). Hence, even
though Yahweh God's creation in 2:7 is specifically a man, i.e.,
an individual male, he is at the same time a symbol of humanity in general (older usage "man") and perhaps of all males
(man).

The proper name Adam (definition 5) also illustrates the
symbolic meaning of 'adam in this story. "Adam" was not really
a proper name in ancient Israel. It does not follow the patterns
that ancient Israelites used to form their names, and no one else
in the Bible is named Adam. It is obviously derived from the
word 'adam and is entirely symbolic. Just as in John Bunyan's
Pilgrim's Progress the hero, "Christian," is the symbol for every
Christian, so Adam is "Everyone" or "Everyman." The name
"Eve" is also symbolic, as we will see momentarily.

The symbolic meaning of Adam fits with the nature of the
creation story in Genesis 2—3 as a whole, which is etiological.
An etiology is a story that is invented to explain the origin of
something—a name, a place, a custom, or even a geological for-

mation. Genesis 2—3 explains the origins of many things. It answers a number of "why" questions, like those which children ask: Why do we wear clothes? Why do snakes crawl? Why do we have to work hard for a living? Why do women have pain in childbirth? Why do we die? Perhaps the best example of an etiology in this story is in 2:24. After the man's expression of delight at the creation of woman, the narrator adds, "Therefore, a man leaves his father and his mother and cleaves to his wife and they become one flesh." The story in chapter 2 and this verse in particular explain why there are two sexes that are so similar by virtue of both being human, yet also very different. The story further explains the attraction between the sexes, and v. 24 is often referred to as an etiology for marriage.

In light of the etiological nature of Genesis 2—3, it is striking that they contain no reference to or explanation of the different races. Adam and Eve are described as the parents of all people. This point is explicitly made for Eve, whose name comes from the Hebrew word for life, so that she is the "mother of all living" (3:20). The story embraces the idea of equality and fraternity among all people, regardless of race. Since all are descended from one couple, all are related, all are a part of one another. The variant account in Genesis 1 does not contradict this idea. While its portrait of creation differs, it also seems to reflect a sense of equality, in that God creates not just one couple but all people at one time. Again, it says nothing about racial distinctions.

The details of the story in chapters 2—3 do allow the reader to deduce Adam's and Eve's "racial" identity. First and foremost, of course, they are members of the human race. But 2:10–14 situates the Garden of Eden in the region of Mesopotamia (between the Tigris and Euphrates Rivers, roughly modern Iraq). Though the story does not say so explicitly, one would assume that the first couple were typically Middle Eastern or Mediterranean in the writer's imagination—olive-skinned and swarthy with black hair. They would not have been seen as "black," since the story is not set in Africa. But they certainly were not "white," or European, as depicted by most (especially Renaissance) artists.

The So-Called
Curse of Ham (Gen. 9:18–27)

The story in 9:18–27 is a strange one and is closely connected in some ways with the genealogy in chapter 10. Noah's three sons are referred to in 9:18–19, and in the next chapter all the peoples of the known earth are traced back to them. We will consider this in more detail momentarily. The story proper begins in 9:20 with the mention of Noah as now a vinedresser, who becomes drunk from the fruit of his agricultural labor (v. 21). These verses are an allusion to the meaning of the name Noah and the pun on it in 5:29. There, Noah's father, Lamech, gives him the name Noah, saying, "This one will bring us *comfort* from our labor and the toil of our hands from the ground which Yahweh has cursed." Noah's name is here related to the word for "comfort" or "relief," and the comfort he brings comes from the vine. This comfort has nothing to do with the flood but rather alludes to Noah's legacy as the inventor of wine. This is his role in 9:20–21.

But the story then takes an unexpected turn. As a result of his intoxication, Noah lies naked in his tent where his son Ham sees him (9:21–22). It was regarded as shameful for a son to see his father's genitals (which is the meaning of "nakedness" in v. 22). Some interpreters have even suggested that Ham's offense involved more than just looking at his unclothed father. They point to the laws in Leviticus 18, which forbid incest, which is described idiomatically as "uncovering the nakedness" of various close relatives. Whatever the exact nature of Ham's deed, it was seen as an embarrassment and insult to Noah. That is why Noah's other sons, Shem and Japheth, take precautions when they cover Noah so as not to view his private parts (9:23). It is also why Noah utters the curse (9:24–27) when he awakes and discovers what Ham has done. The curse, however, is not laid upon Ham, the offender, but rather on his son, Canaan. And herein, for all its strangeness, lies the key to understanding the purpose of this passage.

Before discussing what this passage is, it is worthwhile to show what it is not. It is not a curse on Africans or black people. In order to see how this interpretation arose, it is necessary to glance at chapter 10. The genealogy in that chapter is often called the "table of nations." It is a list of the peoples and nations of the world known at the time of the writer. Its obvious intention is to assign all known peoples an origin, in genealogical terms, from one of Noah's sons. In other words, it seeks to demonstrate how the world was repopulated after the flood from Noah's descendants through his three sons. Now, there is no completely reliable rationale to explain how the nations and peoples are partitioned among the three sons. However, they do seem generally to follow geographic divisions. The descendants of Japheth are mainly situated in the western Mediterranean. Javan (10:2), for example, is Greece. Rodanim (v. 4) is the island of Rhodes; Kittim is Cypress; and Tarshish is a port on the southern coast of Spain.

The "genealogies" of Ham and Shem attest a good deal of confusion. Ham's "descendants" seem to be areas under Egyptian control or influence. Cush refers to the area south of Egypt known as Nubia, or today as Ethiopia. Misrayim is the Hebrew name for Egypt and is translated as such in some English Bibles. Put is Libya, and Canaan is Palestine. The further delineation of Cush, in verses 7–12, includes Nimrod, Babel, Erech, Accad, Shinar, Nineveh, and Calah—all places in Mesopotamia, which should fall within Shem's line, along with Asshur (= Assyria, v. 22), Aram (= Syria, v. 22), and others. The confusion has probably been caused by the fact that "Cush" has more than one meaning. While it generally means Nubia, it can also refer to southern Mesopotamia, where the Kassites (whose name sounds like "Cush" in Hebrew) once ruled.

Two points of importance for our study emerge from surveying this rather confusing situation in chapter 10. First, the three sons of Noah are not to be regarded as the progenitors of the three great races of the modern world (Asian, Negroid, and Caucasian). Genesis 10 reflects a very circumscribed view of the world: the writer's knowledge is basically limited to the Mediterranean, Asia Minor and Turkey, the Middle East, and northern Africa. There is no mention of any east Asian peoples or countries. The places that are included were inhabited by people of Negroid or Caucasian origin, but they are not distinguished by race. Thus, Ethiopians (Cush), Egyptians, Libyans (Put), and the peoples of Canaan are all regarded as "brothers" (10:6). Secondly, the specific curse in 9:25–27 cannot refer to black or Negroid people. It is not Cush who is cursed, not even Ham, but Canaan and his descendants, who have no ethnic ties with

Africa. The attempts to justify slavery or oppression of black people based on this passage are obviously erroneous and the product of a kind of modern racism that the Bible neither reflects nor supports.

What then is the function of this story? One must admit that the curse of Canaan does participate in a sort of racism—the enslavement of an ethnic group. The curse of Canaan is another etiology. It explains how the Israelites displaced the Canaanites in the land and justifies the stories about Israelites subduing and subjugating them. We will consider these stories in later chapters. However, it is worth observing now that the Bible's way of telling this story seems to undercut this curse even as it recounts it. For one thing, the curse comes not from God but from a man, Noah. And while Noah is certainly a great hero in the story of the Flood, the narrative in 9:20–27 casts him in an unsavory role as a drunkard who exposes himself. In addition, the curse, for all the danger and evil it represents, is in a sense quite unreal. There was never any full-scale enslavement of Canaanites by Israel. In fact, the distinction between the two is not entirely clear historically. The Israelites were themselves originally a part of Canaanite society and developed into a nation from within Canaan. The Bible's account of the "conquest of Canaan" reflects this when it describes Canaanites such as Rahab and her family (Joshua 6) and the Gibeonites (Joshua 9) being absorbed into Israel. Most of the time Israelites and Canaanites lived peacefully side by side. For instance, there were individuals in David's army centuries later whom the Bible describes as belonging to different Canaanite ethnic groups (e.g., Uriah the Hittite, 1 Samuel 11). Thus, the Canaanites as they are represented in Noah's curse—as Israel's national enemy—are hypothetical, and in any case certainly cannot be equated with any modern ethnic or racial group.

The Tower of Babel
(11:1–9)

There is one final etiology, in Genesis 11, that is significant for our study. It offers an explanation for the origin of the different languages and cultures of the earth. According to the story, all people once spoke the same language (11:1). Which language it was is not specified. The story also envisions all the earth's inhabitants living and migrating together. In the plain of Shinar, which is Mesopotamia, they decide to build a tower up to heaven (11:2–4). To prevent them from succeeding, Yahweh "confuses" (the Hebrew verb is *balal,* a play on the name Babel) the languages so that the people can no longer understand one another (11:5–7). This, in turn, leads to their scattering abroad throughout the earth, presumably by language groups.

Elements of a diatribe against Mesopotamian religion have been incorporated into the original story. The city where the people attempt to build the tower is identified as Babel, the Hebrew name for Babylon. And the tower itself is to be understood as a ziggurat, the typical, pyramid-shaped temple tower of the ancient Mesopotamians. Two other elements of the story are also important for our present study. First, Yahweh's statement in v. 6 is astounding for its expression of the unlimited potential of human cooperation:

> They are one people who all have the same language, and this is only the beginning of what they will do. Now, nothing they propose to do will be impossible for them.

People working together can accomplish anything! The story implies that even Yahweh is intimidated by this potential and therefore confuses the languages.

The second important aspect of the story for a study of racism is the reason people are separated from one another. Some modern interpreters have found a rationale for apartheid in this story, and it is true that God separates people here. But the real cause of the separation is sin, in particular, inordinate pride. Division between people is contrary to God's initial plan and only enters the world as punishment for sin. It is, therefore, an evil. In a future lesson on Acts we will see that Luke, its author, reflects on the Tower of Babel story in his account of the beginning of the church. When the disciples preach in different languages on the day of Pentecost (Acts 2) the episode conveys a theological message: through Christ, in the church, God heals the divisions between people that sin brought into the world.

2

"All the Families of the Earth"

Election and Blessing in Genesis 12—26

It was called SNCC—the Student Nonviolent Coordinating Committee—and in 1964 it planned "Freedom Summer" in Mississippi. The main purpose of the project was to register black people to vote. Student volunteers—mostly white and mostly from the North—canvassed mainly rural areas in the state. The students received training in Ohio before heading south. SNCC's philosophy was strictly nonviolent; participants were taught to be prepared for various kinds of violence and how to respond nonviolently to any violence they might encounter. It was a philosophy based on Christian principles, as taught by Dr. Martin Luther King Jr. and other ministers. Sometimes the students who trained or traveled held brief devotionals, although most of them were not particularly religious. On June 20, the first wave of trained students left for Mississippi. Among them were Andrew Goodman, 22, James Chaney, 21, and Michael Schwerner, 24. The three disappeared the next day. Their corpses were found about six weeks later. All three had been shot; Chaney, who was black, had been savagely beaten. During those six weeks and after the discovery of the bodies, the devotional periods and the prayers during them increased dramatically in length and intensity as more students "got religion."

One of the root causes of racism is fear of what is different or "foreign." This fear of the "other" is called xenophobia, and as the name indicates it is an unreasonable fear. Usually the "other" is quite similar to "us." Because it is a paranoia, the fear can lead to unreasonable actions, and we inflict the hurt that "we" so much feared from the "other." In this chapter, we will consider several episodes from the life of Abraham, who feared the "other," unnecessarily as it turned out, and responded with deceit and trickery rather than with faith in God. Along the way, we will also explore God's reason for choosing Abraham and God's interest in the nonelect.

The "Patriarchal Promise"

The election of Israel as God's chosen people begins with Abram, who is called in Genesis 12:1–3 to leave his homeland for a journey to a place that is unknown to him, but that Yahweh promises to show him. There are other promises as well:

> I will make you a great nation. I will bless you and make your name great so that you will become a blessing. I will bless those who bless you and curse those who curse you, and all the families of the earth will bless themselves by you [or be blessed through you].

The Abraham and Sarah stories are full of irony. God promises to make Abram into a great nation, but he remains childless for most of his life. In his old age, when his "son of the promise," Isaac, is born of Sarah (Genesis 17), his name is changed from Abram, understood as "exalted father," to Abraham, taken to mean "father of a multitude."[3] The change is highly ironic, for the "father of a multitude" and his wife still have only one son, and at one point (Genesis 22) he is even told to sacrifice that son. When Abraham dies (Gen. 25:7–11), Isaac is barely married—and to a "barren" woman (25:21). Later in chapter 12 (12:7; cf. 13:14–15) Yahweh also promises to give all the land of Canaan to Abram's descendants. But he remains a "resident alien" in Canaan all his life, wandering from place to place (cf. 12:4–9), and, again ironically, he dies owning only the cave in which he and Sarah are buried—a cave that he purchased himself at an exorbitant price (Genesis 23). He is promised that those who bless him will be blessed and those who curse him will be cursed and that other peoples will bless themselves by him (or be blessed through him). But his dealings with other peoples do not usually result in their benefit, even when they do him no harm, as we shall see. Finally, because of his obedience to God's commands to leave his homeland and to sacrifice his only son, Abraham is reputed to be a man of great faith. But again we shall see that in several episodes of the story his words and actions attest incredulity rather than faith.

The promise to Abram in 12:1–3 is also an election formula. By it, God singles out Abram and his descendants for special blessing. The formula is repeated in turn to Isaac (26:3–4) and Jacob (28:13–14) and is recalled when God chooses Moses to lead his people out of Egyptian slavery (Ex. 3:6, 13–16; 6:2–9). An important element of this promise is the statement:

> All the nations [or families] of the earth will bless themselves by you and your descendants [or be blessed through you and your descendants].

Originally, this part of the promise probably meant that Abraham and his heirs would be the model by which other nations would pronounce blessings. In other words, the translation "bless themselves by you" is the more correct. Still, the promise does say that those who bless Abraham also bless themselves. And the Joseph story in Genesis 37—50 provides an example of the nations' being blessed through a descendant of Abraham and Sarah, since Joseph saves the world from famine. Moreover, some parts of the Bible, especially in Isaiah (9:2; 42:6; 49:6; 60:1–3), speak of Israel as a "light to the nations," that is, the means through which all peoples come to know Yahweh. The writers of these parts would interpret this promise to Abraham as reflecting an interest in all peoples of the earth. In this view, the election of Abraham and Israel is God's means by which to bless all the world. Thus, even though universal blessing was probably not intended in the original promise to Abraham, it was interpreted this way within the Bible itself.

The "Wife/Sister" Stories
(Gen. 12:10–20; 20:1–18)

Two episodes in the narratives about Abraham and Sarah are slightly different versions of the same story pattern. A third instance of the pattern occurs for Isaac and Rebekah in 26:6–11.

The versions in chapters 12 and 26 are explicitly related to each other and were likely written by the same author. Isaac and Rebekah's move to Gerar in 26:1 is occasioned by a famine that is compared to the famine that brought about Abram and Sarai's move to Egypt in 12:10. The version in chapter 20 was written later and borrows elements from each of the other two. The basic plot of the story in all three versions is as follows: The patriarch and matriarch journey to a foreign land. The patriarch is afraid for his safety because his wife is beautiful, so he lies or persuades her to lie on his behalf by telling the people of the land and/or their king that she is his sister. In the first two versions (chapters 12 and 20), the king of the land adds Sarai/Sarah to his harem. In all three versions, the king eventually finds out the woman's true identity and confronts the patriarch. In the Isaac version (chapter 26), the king's marriage to Rebekah is preempted by his recognition of her true relationship to Isaac, which is expressed by a pun on his name: He sees Isaac "fondling" (from Hebrew *tsaḥaq*, the same root as *yitsḥaq*, "Isaac") Rebekah (26:8).

The patriarch's lie attests his lack of faith in God to protect him. But what is especially striking for our study is that in all three versions of this story the patriarch's xenophobia is unfounded. He has no reason to fear the foreigners, who actually turn out to be more righteous than he. The pharaoh in 12:10–20 marries Sarai (takes her into his house, 12:15) and enriches Abram for her sake (12:16). When he discovers the truth he sends the couple away without harming them (12:17–20). In 26:10 Abimelech points out to Isaac the moral peril that his lie might have caused: "One of the people might easily have lain with your wife, and you would have brought guilt upon us!" Moral concerns are especially pronounced in the version in chapter 20. The writer (20:4a) points out that Abimelech did not approach Sarah and thus cannot have committed adultery. Abimelech himself (20:4b) affirms his innocence. And God (20:5) admits that he acted "in the integrity of [his] heart." It is Abraham, not Abimelech, who has done "things that should not be done" (v. 9). Abraham's fear that "there is no reverence for God in this place" (v. 11) has certainly proven not to be the case. The foreigners demonstrate a greater reverence for God and fairer treatment of others than the elect patriarch. In these stories, the "nations" are more righteous than the chosen.

Hagar and Ishmael
(Gen. 16:1–16; 21:8–21)

Hagar's Flight (Gen. 16:1–16)

Yahweh's promise to Abram that he would engender a great nation encounters several obstacles as the story proceeds. The first of these is that Abram's wife, Sarai, is "barren," that is, unable to conceive children. In Genesis 16, Sarai comes up with a way to help Yahweh keep the promise. She offers her hand-maid Hagar, as a surrogate to bear an heir to Abraham. The social and cultural institutions presupposed in this story are so different from those of today that they demand special explanation. One of these institutions was slavery. Hagar was Sarai's slave. Slavery was common in the ancient world, but it was different from the slavery practiced in nineteenth-century United States. Ancient slavery was not the fruit of racism. Slaves in antiquity were either captives from wars or persons forced by debt to sell themselves. This certainly does not make the institution any less insidious, from a modern perspective, but it is important for our present purposes to make clear that Hagar's status as a slave had nothing to do with her racial or ethnic identity. Female slaves often came with their mistresses in a marriage. Marriages were arranged as matters of legal contracts. Some marriage contracts preserved from ancient Mesopotamia specify what appears to be implicit in the Bible's story about Hagar. The wife, according to such contracts, was responsible for providing an heir to her husband. If she could not bear one herself, she was to supply a female slave who could do so. The contracts and laws about such arrangements also contain other specifications that are important background to the biblical account, as we shall see below.

The careful reader will notice that it is Sarai, not Abram, who proposes the surrogacy of Hagar (16:2). It seems odd to modern readers that a wife would volunteer to share her husband with another woman. Sarai's language suggests, however, that she is under legal (and certainly social) constraint. When she proposes that Abram have relations with Hagar she adds, "Perhaps I will *be built up* through her" (16:2). The expression in italics is sometimes translated, rather blandly, "obtain children." But it seems to have fuller connotations, such as "fulfill my legal responsibility." At any rate, Abram and Hagar conceive a child (16:4). The laws about such relationships prohibit a pregnant slave girl from treating her infertile mistress with contempt. But this is a natural reaction, and it is Hagar's response in the story (16:4). Sarai blames Abram (16:5), which again may seem rather strange to the modern reader, but since Sarai has given Hagar to Abram, she is now his property, and Sarai's only recourse is through him. Ancient laws also forbade the abusive treatment of a pregnant slave by her infertile mistress that Sarai now heaps upon Hagar. But again, this reaction is natural. It is this mistreatment that leads Hagar to flee (16:6).

Hagar is obviously on her way back home to Egypt via the "way of Shur" (16:7), when an angel of Yahweh meets her at a well (16:7–8). The scene is remarkable in several respects. First of all, unlike other such stories, especially the one in Genesis 21, in which the angel addresses a situation of crisis or need, in this case the angel simply tells Hagar to return to Sarai (16:9). This is even more unusual in light of the episode's ending (see below). Second, in verse 10 the angel reiterates for Hagar an element of the "patriarchal" promise: "I will greatly increase your descendants so that they will be too many to count." This is the only time in the Bible that an element of this promise is given to anyone other than one of the patriarchs, Abraham, Isaac, or Jacob. Not even Sarah or any of the other mothers of Israel have the promise given to them. Yet here it is given to the Egyptian slave, Hagar. The promise is made in reference to Ishmael, the son Hagar is to bear. Just as Yahweh later promises to bless Isaac and his descendants, so he will also bless Ishmael and his line. Isaac may be the son of promise and Israel the chosen people, but Yahweh also cares for the nonelect, for Ishmael and his Arab descendants. Verse 12 contains an etiology for the origin and nature of the Ishmaelites. They are portrayed as tough denizens of the wilderness who survive against and at odds with the surrounding peoples.

Hagar's Dismissal
(Gen. 21:8–21)

One would next expect the passage in Genesis 16 to go on to narrate Ishmael's birth and to describe how he and his mother survived in the wilderness to found the new, promised nation. But it is another remarkable feature of this text that the story ends with Hagar's return according to the angel's order. Ishmael's birth is recounted (16:15–16), but there is no word yet about his becoming a nation. That is left to the end of the second, very similar story about Hagar and Ishmael in 21:8–21. In fact, the return of Hagar at the end of chapter 16 seems to be the product of narrative strategy to enhance the story's tension and present one final obstacle to the succession of the son of promise.

Sarai's plan to "be built up" through Hagar and Abram's compliance with it may be seen as their effort to help God. They had given up on having a child between themselves, had lost faith in God's fulfilling the promise in the usual way. So they decided to give God a helping hand through an expediency available in their culture. Their help, however, quickly turned into a hindrance when God's original plan went forward. This was especially true where Sarah was concerned. At a feast given by Abraham on the day of Isaac's weaning (21:8), when he would have been two or three years old, Sarah came to full realization of the problem posed by Ishmael. Verse 9 says that Sarah saw Ishmael "laughing." The word is a form of the Hebrew verb *tsahaq*, "to laugh," which is used elsewhere in the story (e.g., 21:6) as a pun on Isaac's name. This leads Sarah to insist that Abraham drive out Hagar and Ishmael. But how could the mere sight of Ishmael laughing lead Sarah to such drastic action? This problem has apparently motivated the Septuagint, the Greek translation of the Hebrew Bible, to supply the words "with [or "at"] her son Isaac" at the end of the verse. Thus, Ishmael is seen as laughing at Isaac or mocking him in some way, and this angers Sarah so that she demands Hagar's dismissal. A better interpretation may be simply to follow the Hebrew text and perceive its reading as the narrator's clever device: Sarah's glimpse of Ishmael "laughing" reminds her that he is replacing her son, Isaac, as Abraham's heir. Hence, her insistence that Abraham "drive out the slave woman with her son" is explicitly motivated by her desire that "the son of the slave woman . . . not inherit with my son Isaac" (21:10).

Now the marriage contracts and legal texts mentioned earlier that deal with this sort of situation specifically prohibit driving out or disinheriting a slave woman's son if he is the firstborn and the wife later bears a son. This may explain Abraham's distress at Sarah's demand (21:11). He no doubt felt affection for Ishmael as his son, and was loath to send him away for that reason. But he was also reluctant to do so because such an act would be a violation of social and perhaps legal convention. He complies with Sarah's demand only after God tells him to, at the same time revealing to him that Isaac is to be his real heir, the son of the promise (21:12). God also makes another promise to Abraham (21:13). It is the same promise Yahweh made to Hagar first—that he would make of her son a great nation, just as of Isaac. The chosen son and the chosen people are not the only ones to receive God's blessing.

Abraham sends Hagar and Ishmael away in the early morning (21:14). He gives her food and water, knowing that her journey will be long and perilous. She wanders in the wilderness of Beer-sheba, again on her way toward Egypt. This is hot, dry, barren land, and her water soon runs out. This time there is a crisis and a real need for the angel of God to appear (21:17). There is some confusion in this account about the age of Ishmael. Following the chronology of these stories, Abraham was eighty-six years old when Ishmael was born (16:16) and one hundred at Isaac's birth (21:5). If Isaac was weaned at two years of age (21:8), then Ishmael would have been about sixteen when he and his mother were sent away—much too large for Hagar to carry on her shoulder (21:14) or to cast under a bush (21:15). All of this suggests that 21:14–21 reflects the original ending of the story in chapter 16, before the narrator created two versions of the story for dramatic reasons. Be that as it may, Hagar leaves her son because she cannot bear to watch him die (21:16).

Now comes the ending we expected in chapter 16. The angel responds to Hagar's desperate need by showing her a well, which was either a new creation or which she had not previously noticed (21:19). The well in this account is not merely the setting of the tale as it is in chapter 16 but is integral to the plot of the story. Before showing her the well, the angel reassures her of God's protection and guidance by reiterating the promise, though in a briefer form, that Ishmael will become a great nation (21:18). It is then that the story can end by relating that God blessed Ishmael in the wilderness. The fulfillment of the promise is implicit here but becomes explicit in 25:12–18, where the genealogy of the Ishmaelite tribes is given.

The Bible portrays the "Ishmaelites" as traders who lived

and trafficked between southern Palestine and Egypt, especially in the Sinai peninsula, which includes the wilderness of Paran, where Ishmael settled (Gen. 21:21). The stories about Ishmael are eponymous in nature. This means that Ishmael represents or stands for the nation. It is no accident that the Ishmaelite territory was between Palestine and Egypt, and it may be that Hagar is described as an Egyptian in order to accord with the geographical locations of the principal characters in the story. It is the relationships between those characters that are important for our story. Isaac is the elect son of Abraham—chosen by God to be the one through whom the patriarchal promise is fulfilled. As Isaac represents the Israelites, so Ishmael represents Israel's neighbors, the Arabs. The Bible depicts them as brothers. More than that, the Bible portrays both groups as recipients of God's promises and objects of God's love and concern.

The texts we have surveyed in the Abraham and Sarah stories also contain broader lessons for our consideration. In the wife/sister stories, the "foreign nations," both inside of Palestine (Gerar) and outside (Egypt), are portrayed quite positively. Indeed, their fear of God and immediate response to divine commands contrasts not only with Abraham's fears about them but also with his own lack of faith, to say nothing of the contrast between their concerns for morality and fairness and his rather callous betrayal of their trust. Finally, while the stories of Abraham and Sarah focus on the concept of election—the choosing first of Abraham and then of Isaac—at least one strain of interpretation within the Bible saw God's ultimate goal as universal blessing ("By you and your descendants will all the nations of the earth be blessed"). By this understanding, election is not an end in itself but merely a means to an end that includes all races.

part two

The Nature of Israel

3

"You Must Utterly Destroy Them"

Holy War in Deuteronomy and the Deuteronomistic History

Addie Mae Collins, Denise McNair, Carole Robertson, and Cynthia Wesley—they were not much younger than I was in 1963. On the morning of September 15 they were doing what I and thousands of other children across the country were doing. They were getting ready for church. They had attended Sunday school and were in the basement of the church building changing into their choir robes to sing in the sanctuary. A church building is called a sanctuary—it's supposed to be a place of safety, a refuge from the outside world. But on that particular Sunday the Sixteenth Street Baptist Church in Birmingham, Alabama, was not safe. At 10:19 fifteen sticks of dynamite blew the changing room apart and rocked the church. A few blocks away, Robert "Dynamite Bob" Chambliss, a Klansman who would be convicted of the crime fourteen years later, stood watching. Twenty or so were injured, four were dead—Addie Mae Collins, Denise McNair, Carole Robertson, and Cynthia Wesley.

The greatest horrors of racism are the acts of violence done to children. Our topic in this chapter is the mandate in the book of Deuteronomy and the books that follow for the Israelites to engage in such violence. They were told to conquer and annihilate the Canaanites—men, women, and children. This was one of the strains of exclusivism that were present in ancient Israel, in spite of the lessons about God's universal love in Genesis.

Our task will be to try to set it in its historical, cultural, and literary context.

The Practice of Holy War

The name Deuteronomy means "second law." The book consists of a speech or speeches of Moses in which he reviews the law (Deut. 1:5) for the people shortly before his death (34:1–8). The setting of the book is the "plains of Moab" east of the Jordan River (1:5). The people of Israel are camped there, poised to enter the promised land of Canaan. Because of a past offense, Moses is not allowed to enter with them (1:37). He can only look upon it from the distant Mount Nebo before he dies (32:48–52). In his speeches he tells the people how they are to take the land and then live in it according to the law that they have received from God.

The order as to how they are to treat the seven peoples native to the land (7:1), which I group together for the sake of convenience as "Canaanites," is harsh and calls for complete annihilation: "You must utterly destroy them. You shall not make a covenant with them or show them mercy" (7:2). This commandment is especially alarming for modern readers who have seen the horrifying effects of "ethnic cleansing" in our own century. We have come to regard such policies and tactics on the part of any military as unjustifiable and unacceptable. The discussion that follows is not meant to justify the mandate in Deuteronomy or to explain it away. As mentioned in the Preface, we must admit that the Bible contains instances of national and ethnic exclusivism, of which this commandment in Deuteronomy is one example. Our task in this chapter will be to attempt to understand something of the context in which it arose. Then, both here and in subsequent chapters, we will explore the responses to it within the Bible itself.

The Hebrew word for the annihilation the Israelites were to effect against their Canaanite enemies is *herem*. It is used in the Old Testament, as in Deuteronomy 7:2, for the devotion of a group of people, such as a city, to destruction. The key element in its meaning is "devotion." The city is actually devoted to Yahweh. As in the case of Jericho (Josh. 7:17–18), this means that the people and the animals of the city are to be executed according to God's holy purpose. The property of the city is holy in that sense, and therefore is also to be destroyed rather than taken as plunder. Only the valuable metals—gold, silver, and bronze—are retained for deposit into the treasury for Yahweh (7:19), for they also belong to Yahweh.

The practice of *herem* was not unique to Israel. It is mentioned in a well-known inscription from ancient Moab, the country on the other side of the Jordan River from Israel, and similar practices were carried out by other countries in the ancient Middle East. In this inscription, the Moabite king, Mesha, describes how he devoted cities that he conquered to the Moabite god, Chemosh. The exact origin of the practice is not known, but the Mesha inscription and the biblical passages suggest that it may have been a way of avenging a particular "insult" to a god or the god's people. In the Old Testament world, each nation had its own god, and the nation was regarded as the heritage and property of its god. A national army might "devote" to destruction a "foreign" group of people who lived inside the territory of their god but who did not worship that god.

This ideology is given particular religious significance in Deuteronomy's mandate. The command to devote the Canaanite peoples to destruction was not applicable to all non-Israelites. Deuteronomy 20:10–18 distinguishes between warfare against the cities of the Canaanite peoples and warfare against cities that are "far from you," that is, outside of Canaan. For the latter, the Israelites are to offer terms of peace (20:10). Then, if the city refuses the terms, the Israelites are to kill the males but may take the women, children, and property as spoils of war (20:12–14). Non-Israelites who were "resident aliens" in Israel (often translated "sojourners") are mentioned in several laws in Deuteronomy. Along with widows, orphans, and other groups, they are especially vulnerable to abuse, and so the law makes provision for special protection (24:17–18). They receive some of the tithe collected for the underprivileged (14:28–29; 27:12) and are allowed to glean the fields for food (24:19–22). In short, "foreigners" who reside in Israel have most of the same rights and responsibilities as citizens (16:9–12; 24:14–15).

The command to devote the Canaanites to destruction has an explicitly religious rationale. They would be a "snare" to the Israelites, by leading them into the worship of other gods (Deut. 7:4, 16). They are to be destroyed "so that they will not teach you to do according to all the abominations which they have done for their gods" (20:18). This is such a danger that the Israelites must even be careful not to be tempted after the Canaanites are gone (12:29–31). They must destroy all the Canaanite worship places along with their altars and idols (12:1–3). The punishment of death is not reserved only for the Canaanites but is also to be exacted upon Israelite cities that forsake Yahweh for the worship of other gods (13:12–18). All the inhabitants of such a city, including the animals, are to be killed (13:15) and the city with all its property burned, never to be rebuilt (13:16). An individual who is proven guilty of apostasy is to be executed by stoning in order to "purge the evil from your midst" (17:2–7). The same applies to persons who engage in other types of religious practice associated with the Canaanite peoples (18:9–14). Thus, the "devotion" of the Canaanites and the exclusivism of Deuteronomy is religious rather than ethnic in motivation.

The Setting of the Deuteronomistic History

The book of Deuteronomy is the first volume of what most Old Testament scholars consider to be a multivolume work in the Bible on the history of Israel. This work is known as the Deuteronomistic History and incorporates the books of Deuteronomy, Joshua, Judges, 1 and 2 Samuel, and 1 and 2 Kings. The policy of annihilating the Canaanites in the Old Testament is a product of, and for all practical purposes is limited to, the Deuteronomistic History. Deuteronomy establishes the mandate for this policy, as we have seen, and the instances of the implementation of the policy in Israel's history are reported in the other books. So it will be instructive to consider the setting of the Deuteronomistic History before we move to a survey of those instances.

The final chapter of the Deuteronomistic History, 2 Kings 25, describes the destruction of Jerusalem and the Temple by the Babylonian army in 586 B.C. The Deuteronomistic History as we now have it was obviously written or compiled after this date, though there may have been earlier editions. The important point for our present topic is that the Deuteronomistic History deals with the identity crisis of the people of Israel in the light or the wake of the turbulent events at the end of its kingdom. Two other events were of crucial importance for the monarchy in the Deuteronomistic History's presentation. The first was the division of the united kingdom following Solomon into the two nations of Israel and Judah. The second was the destruction of Israel by the Assyrians in 701 B.C. Judah's destruction then came in 586. The author(s) of the Deuteronomistic History attributed all three disasters to the sin of worshiping other gods. Solomon's foreign wives led him astray, and the kingdom was divided as a result. Israel and then Judah in turn forsook Yahweh, and their respective destructions ensued. Thus, for the Deuteronomistic History, Israel's continued existence was bound up with its religious identity as the people of Yahweh. Its author(s) sought to (re)establish Israel's identity through a series of religious "exclusives." Israel was to worship Yahweh exclusively, and the worship was to take place exclusively at the Temple in Jerusalem. Foreign gods were a threat to this exclusivity, and therefore to Israel's identity and existence. But an even greater threat was the gods, like Baal, who were at home in Canaan and closely tied people's thinking to the cycles that brought fertility to land and animals. The author(s) of the Deuteronomistic History particularly wanted to distance Yahweh and Israel from these Canaanite gods and the religion associated with them.

When the Deuteronomistic History (including the mandate to destroy the Canaanites in Deuteronomy 7) was written, the different Canaanite peoples as separate ethnic groups had long since disappeared from the land. For the most part, they had simply been absorbed within Israel (see chapter 4 of this book). But the fertility religion involving Baal and other gods that had been associated with the land of Canaan for centuries still thrived—largely among Israelites! The prophets in Israel going back to the eighth century had condemned this worship, and now the author(s) of the Deuteronomistic History, in the same tradition, also condemned it. The Canaanites and their religion were to be removed from the land. But in fact those Canaanite groups no longer existed; they were "straw figures" that the Deuteronomistic historian(s) set up for the purpose of consolidating the people of Israel in religious unity. Some scholars have even suggested that the reason for giving the rules of war against the now fictional "Canaanites" was to prevent the execution of *herem* against real peoples who were alive at the time Deuteronomy was written. None of this diminishes the horror of the *idea* of genocide that is mandated in Deuteronomy 7, but it does point out the mandate's unreal nature.

Carrying Out the Conquest

Jericho (Joshua 6—7)

The Deuteronomistic History recounts several instances of carrying out the "devotion" of Canaanite cities. The best-known case is that of Jericho. After seven days of the Isrealite army marching around the city, Yahweh collapsed its wall and gave it over to Israelite conquest (6:1–16, 20). Joshua announces that the city is devoted to Yahweh, so that all the people and animals within it are to be killed and the property destroyed or turned over to the sacred treasury (6:17–19). The army follows Joshua's order (6:21), but there are two important exceptions. First, Rahab and all those who are in her house are preserved (6:17). In the next chapter, this book will examine Rahab's story as a response to the policy of "devoting" the Canaanites. She is an essential part of the conquest of Jericho; without her help the spies would not have succeeded, and Jericho might not have fallen. For the moment, however, it is enough to observe that keeping Rahab and her household alive, however many they were, undermines the "devotion" of Jericho and prevents it from being complete.

Another person, named Achan, also prevents the total "devotion" of Jericho, though in a very different way from Rahab. His story is in Joshua 7. By taking some of the spoil of the city, he violates the order to "devote" it to Yahweh (7:1, 20–21). His mistake brings about the defeat of Israel and the loss of thirty-six of its soldiers in the battle for the small town of Ai (7:2–5), to say nothing of the disheartening effect it has on Joshua and the army (7:5–9). Only after Achan's sin is confessed (7:16–21), and atoned for by obliterating him, his family, and his property (7:22–26), are the Israelites able to return to Ai and take it (8:1–23).

The Rest of Canaan (Joshua 10—11)

Joshua 8:24–29 reports that the Israelites slaughtered all the inhabitants of Ai, hung their king, and took the cattle and property as spoil. Beginning in 10:28, chapters 10—11 recount the similar treatment of other Canaanite cities in summary fashion. The final result comes in 11:23:

Joshua took all the land according to all that Yahweh had told Moses, and Joshua gave it as an inheritance to Israel according to their allotments by their tribes.

Despite this overview and Joshua's conquest of key cities, there were still plenty of Canaanites living in the land, so that the conquest of Canaan and the annihilation of its native population was not thorough. First of all, the story of the conquest is interrupted in chapters 9—10 by that of the Gibeonites, who fool the Israelites into making a treaty with them, so that they continue to live in the land. We will treat this story in more detail in the next chapter. Then, in the account of the division of the land that follows in chapters 12—24, several peoples are mentioned who, like the Gibeonites, were not destroyed but remained in the land living side by side with the Israelites. These include: Geshurites and Maacathites (13:13), Anakim (14:12), Jebusites (15:63), and Canaanites (16:10; 17:12). The list of unconquered Canaanites is even longer in the first chapter of Judges. In most cases, the Israelites are said to have enslaved the Canaanite natives but not destroyed them or driven them out of the land.

In part, this situation corresponds with the perspective of Deuteronomy 7:22, which ascribes the gradual removal of the Canaanites to Yahweh's intentional plan to prevent the wild animals from becoming too numerous. But the author(s) of the Deuteronomistic History explained the fall of Israel as the result of the continued Canaanite presence. The Canaanites led the Israelites astray religiously, and their apostasy eventually brought on national disasters as punishment. For whatever reasons, as with the conquest of Jericho, the ordered annihilation of the Canaanites ultimately proved unworkable. Reality undercut the "ideal."

Saul and the Amalekites (1 Samuel 15)

Deuteronomy 25:17–19 contains a special mandate to destroy the Amalekites, out of revenge for their attack on the people of Israel when they had just come out of Egypt (Ex. 17:8–15). In 1 Samuel 15, Saul is charged with carrying out this mandate and is told to execute *ḥerem* against the Amalekites by killing all their people and animals (15:3). Saul does indeed attack the Amalekites, and destroys all of them except for the king and the best of the livestock (15:7–9). He claims that he saved the animals for sacrifice (15:15), and he may have kept the king alive for a special, ritual execution, along the lines of what Joshua did to the king of Ai (Josh. 8:29).[4] But despite his motives, both Yahweh and Samuel were displeased that he had not carried out to the letter the order to "devote" the Amalekites, by killing them all in the field. Samuel delivered his famous "obedience is better than sacrifice" oracle and promptly announced that Yahweh had rejected Saul as king: "Today Yahweh has torn the kingdom from you and given it to your neighbor who is better than you" (15:28). The neighbor, of course, is David, and this episode of the rejection of Saul leads into the story of David's rise to the throne, which begins in chapter 16. Ironically, a few chapters later, in 1 Samuel 22, Saul executes the "devotion" against Yahweh's own priests when he is convinced that they have conspired with David, of whom Saul has become insanely jealous. Moreover, the Amalekites come back again and again in Saul's life, as the story is now told. It is they who raid Ziklag (1 Samuel 30), and it is an Amalekite who finally kills Saul, according to 2 Samuel 1. Even against the hated Amalekites, the policy of devotion did not work, and actually became Saul's undoing.

In all three of these examples—Jericho, the Canaanites in general, and the Amalekites—the policy of "devotion" to destruction was ineffective. For the author(s) of the Deuteronomistic History this was because the Israelites failed to carry out the "devotion" completely, and this in turn led to their eventual downfall. But a modern reader might suggest that the policy itself was flawed. In subsequent chapters, we will treat the stories of Rahab and the Gibeonites, as well as the book of Ruth, as responses to ethnically exclusivistic interpretations of Deuteronomy's policy of "devotion," if not directly to the policy itself. All these stories and sources agree that there was ethnic diversity within ancient Israel. The responses contend that at least in some cases this was a good thing.

4

"A Mixed Crowd"

The Ethnic Diversity of Ancient Israel

When Israel was in Egypt's land, Let my people go!
Oppressed so hard they could not stand, Let my people go!

Go down, Moses, Way down in Egypt's land.
Tell ole Pharaoh, Let my people go!

"Thus saith the Lord," bold Moses said, "Let my people go!
If not, I'll smite your firstborn dead." Let my people go!

—Traditional spiritual

From cradle to grave, Ida B. Wells-Barnett lived with and fought against racism. Born in 1862 to parents who were slaves, Wells-Barnett was emancipated at the end of the Civil War and lived in the rural South until adulthood. She was educated at Shaw University (now known as Rust College), a school established by the Freedman's Aid Society in Holly Springs, Mississippi. She later took a job as a schoolteacher in Memphis and suffered with black children from the poor and unequal conditions of segregated schools. She lost her job with the city school board in 1890 for speaking out in a newspaper editorial about the "few and utterly inadequate" buildings and the poor training of some of the teachers assigned to those schools. Turning then to journalism full-time, Wells-Barnett served as editor of *The Free Speech*, an early African-American newspaper based in Memphis, which was circulated widely in the South. With great dignity and thoughtfulness, she registered her conviction that blacks were treated unfairly and routinely denied justice. After the deaths of three Memphis friends who were lynched in a racial incident in March of 1892, she heightened her editorial campaign against racism. Wells-Barnett called on African Americans to leave the city that offered no justice for them. In her autobiography, she reports that hundreds left Memphis, including pastors who took whole congregations westward. A white mob destroyed Wells-Barnett's Memphis press in 1892. Out of town at the time, she was warned not to return to Memphis because of threats on her life.

> There is therefore only one thing left that we can do; save our money and leave a town which will neither protect our lives and property, nor give us a fair trial in the courts, but takes us out and murders us in cold blood when accused by white persons.
>
> (Contributed by Susan McLain Sullivan)

Ida B. Wells's life and career remind one of Moses, whom we shall mention in this chapter. Like him, she was a leader and spokesperson for her people against oppression. Like Moses, she called for an exodus from harsh treatment and injustice. She also shared traits with other biblical characters we shall consider here. Like Rahab, she was courageous and insightful, and like one of Moses' wives, she was of African descent.

In chapter 3 we examined a tradition in Deuteronomy and the Deuteronomistic History that mandated annihilating the Canaanites. We suggested that this tradition was part of a concern for religious "purity" from a relatively late date in Israel's history, and that the wholesale annihilation depicted in these texts never actually occurred. Nonetheless, even the idea of "ethnic cleansing" like this is frightening and offensive to modern readers—and rightly so. In fact, other parts of the Bible itself offer a response of sorts that, together with historical considerations, undermines and counters the anti-Canaanite theme. That response is found in the claim that from its beginning the nation of Israel was not ethnically united but incorporated people of various backgrounds, including Canaanites. Indeed, from a historical perspective, the ethnic distinction between Israelites and Canaanites is rather vague.

Moses' Wives

Israel's birth as a nation, according to the Bible, took place at the exodus from Egypt under Moses.

> When Israel was a child I loved him,
> And out of Egypt I called my son.
> (Hos. 11:1)

But the Israel that Moses led out of slavery was not an ethnic unity. Exodus 12:38 mentions a large "mixed crowd" that accompanied the Israelites when they left Egypt. This was a heterogeneous group of people whose ties to Israel were not ethnic but grounded in the common experience of slavery. The Bible pictures these people as being with Israel's ancestors in the exodus from Egypt and eventually becoming absorbed within the new nation itself. In fact, the very name "Hebrew" seems originally to have designated a socioeconomic class rather than an ethnic group.

Moses' own wife could be considered part of this "mixed crowd," though she had not directly experienced bondage in Egypt. Her name was Zipporah, and she was from the land of Midian in the southern Arabian peninsula (modern Saudi Arabia). The wife of Israel's first leader and greatest liberator, therefore, was not an Israelite by ethnic background. But she, like so many others, was incorporated as part of the nation.

There is a story involving Moses' wife that is especially pertinent for our present study. In Numbers 12, Moses' siblings, Aaron and Miriam, question his leadership: "Is it only through Moses that Yahweh has spoken? Has he not also spoken through us?" (12:2). The real reason that they speak against Moses, though, has to do with his marriage to a Cushite woman (12:1). The scant details in this story immediately raise two questions: (1) Who exactly is this Cushite woman? and (2) What is it about her that leads Aaron and Miriam to complain about Moses' leadership? While the story does not address either question directly, its plot does suggest related answers to both.

The issue that surrounds the first question is whether this woman is to be identified with Zipporah. Some scholars have assumed that she is, and have therefore suggested that in addition to its more common designations of Nubia (Ethiopia) and southern Mesopotamia, "Cush" could also refer to an area or

33

clan in Midian. They cite two other passages in support of this suggestion: Habakkuk 3:7 uses the name Cushan in parallel with Midian, so that they could be two names for the same region. But "Cushan" is not exactly the same as Cush and is not attested anywhere else in the Bible, so that its precise meaning is uncertain. The other passage is more compelling. Second Chronicles 21:16 refers to "the Arabs who are near the Cushites." The Cushites here are not likely Nubians, since Nubia was nowhere near Arab peoples. They are also not likely Mesopotamians, since the story deals with Judah and its nearby neighbors.

But even if Cush could refer to an area of Midian, it seems unlikely that the Cushite woman in Numbers 12 is Zipporah. Zipporah has been mentioned by name previously and been called a Midianite, so it would be unusual for her suddenly to be referred to here enigmatically as a Cushite. This appears to be a new marriage for Moses, and the remainder of the story suggests that his Cushite bride was indeed Nubian and therefore black. Moreover, it was evidently because she was black that Aaron and Miriam began to question their brother's leadership. It is in the light of this understanding that Miriam's punishment in the story (12:10–16) makes the most sense. She is afflicted with a skin disease (often interpreted as leprosy) and excluded from the camp for seven days. The text specifically states that she became "as white as snow" (12:10). It is not entirely clear why Miriam alone is punished and not Aaron. Perhaps it was because she was the real instigator of the complaint (note that she is mentioned first in 12:1), or perhaps because she, like Moses' wife, the target of her complaint, was a woman. In either case, her becoming pale white with disease was a particularly appropriate counter to her objection to Moses' black wife.

Clever Canaanites:
Rahab and the Gibeonites

The book of Joshua recounts the execution of the mandate treated in the preceding chapter, to conquer Canaan and annihilate its inhabitants. Joshua's account is clearly idealized, an overview of the constituent parts of the land of Israel. The very next book, Judges, shows that in fact the Canaanites continued to thrive and even dominate in the land claimed by Israel. But even in Joshua's telling of the story, the truth emerges that the complete destruction of the Canaanites was impossible, impractical, and in the end, undesirable.

Rahab

Two stories about the Canaanite presence in Israel stand out. The first is that of the exceptional woman, Rahab. Rahab was a harlot, a prostitute. One must be careful at this point not to read modern moral judgments into the story. There were no paying jobs for women in that ancient society, and prostitution was one of the few means that unmarried women had of sustaining themselves, especially in a city like Jericho. Rahab's description as a harlot says more about her independence and judiciousness in dealing with men than it does about her moral character. However, it also indicates her low socio-economic level and suggests that she was something of an outcast among her own people. Perhaps this is one reason why she helped the Israelite spies.

In Joshua 2:1 the two Israelite spies go to Rahab's house because, as strangers in the city of Jericho, they would be inconspicuous in a prostitute's house. Rahab hides and protects them when the king of the city sends men to arrest them (2:2–7). Before she lets them go, however, she extracts a promise from them to spare her and everyone in her house when the city falls to the Israelites (12:8–14).

The insight and faith ascribed to Rahab in this episode are extraordinary. On the basis of what she has heard about the Israelites and their victories, she has come to believe that Yahweh, their God, is Lord of all the earth (2:10–11). She also says that she knows God will give Jericho and indeed all of Canaan to Israel (2:9). Her insight and faith are the grounds on which she makes the arrangement with the spies to save her own life and that of her family (2:12–14). At the very least one must admire Rahab's astuteness in this affair. A cynical reader might suggest that she hedges her bets. If the Israelites fail in their assault on Jericho and the city survives, she has lost nothing. She convincingly lies to the king's messengers (2:4–5), so that they do not suspect her as an accomplice in the spies' mission. On the other hand, if the Israelites do succeed against Jericho, Rahab has gained everything. But there is more to Rahab's actions than a cynical reading allows. In protecting the spies she risks her own life and shows herself to be a courageous woman. Her faith and good judgment move her to act boldly.

The Israelites, of course, do succeed against Jericho, and when the city falls she is prepared and waiting according to her bargain with the spies (6:22–25). She saves her parents, siblings, and other family members. The story ends by pointing out that she (and presumably her family as well) lived in Israel from then on (6:25). But that is not the last we hear of Rahab in the Bible. According to the genealogy in Matthew 1, Rahab came to occupy a prominent place in Israel as the great-great-grandmother of King David and the ancestress of Jesus. The one-time prostitute from among the despised Canaanites not only played a crucial role in Israel's conquest of the land, but also had a part in engendering Israel's greatest king and the Savior of the world!

The Gibeonites

Gibeon was an ancient and important Canaanite city just north of Jerusalem. According to Joshua 9, its residents acted cleverly to deceive Joshua and the Israelites and to ensure the survival of their city. The Gibeonites were terrified by the tales they heard of Israel's conquests through the power of Yahweh (9:24). Knowing they could not win a military victory, they decided that their one chance for survival was through a ruse. So they sent messengers dressed in old, worn-out clothing with failing provisions as though they had been on a long journey (9:4–5). The messengers told Joshua and the leaders of Israel that they came from a distant country, which had heard, nevertheless, of Israel's military successes and had decided to sue for peace by making a covenant (9:9–11). Joshua and the leaders were so flattered that they immediately agreed to a pact without consulting Yahweh (9:14). When they discovered a short time later who the messengers really were (9:16), they could not destroy them because they had taken oaths by Yahweh not to do so (9:19–20). Instead, the inhabitants of Gibeon and its environs (9:17) were put to work as "hewers of wood and drawers of water," or slaves, for the Israelites (9:21, 27).

The lowly status of the Gibeonites within Israel did not last long, despite the intentions of Joshua and the leaders. Within a few short years, the city became so thoroughly incorporated into

Israel that the tabernacle resided in its sanctuary in the early days of David (1 Chron. 16:39), and it was apparently at this sanctuary that Solomon prayed and received the dream in which Yahweh promised him great wisdom (1 Kings 3:3–15). Nonetheless, Gibeon's citizens were still predominantly the ethnic Canaanites whom Joshua had encountered, as the story in 2 Samuel 21:1–14 shows. Here, David discovers that a famine in Israel is divine punishment for Saul's having violated Joshua's treaty with the Gibeonites, and he negotiates with them to find a solution. The point for our present purposes is that the biblical texts describe Gibeon as an important city of Israel already, within a short time after Joshua's covenant with them. This is not because ethnic Israelites replaced the city's Canaanite inhabitants, but because the Canaanite city was simply absorbed into Israel.

A Melting Pot:
The Reign of David

David is renowned in the Bible for his great military conquests, by which he built an empire for Israel. In view of this reputation it is striking to note how many individuals in the Bible's stories about David are referred to explicitly as members of non-Israelite ethnic groups. To begin with one of the most famous examples, Uriah the Hittite is listed in the "hall of fame" of David's best soldiers (2 Sam. 23:39). He was also extremely loyal to David, as his actions in 2 Samuel 11 show. David's great sin was that he committed adultery with Uriah's wife, Bathsheba, and plotted Uriah's murder. This had nothing to do with Uriah's ethnic designation as a Hittite, but was due entirely to David's failure to control his lust. The Bible uses the term "Hittite" for one of the peoples indigenous to Canaan (e.g., Gen. 15:19–21) whom the Israelites were supposed to obliterate according to Deuteronomy 7:1. Yet it is clear that Uriah had been fully accepted within Israel. He had an Israelite wife and all the privileges of any Israelite citizen. Therefore, Nathan the prophet condemns David's sin against Uriah as completely as he would a similar offense against any Israelite (2 Sam. 12:1–14).

David's most famous individual battle, of course, was the one he fought with the Philistine champion, Goliath. The Philistines were Israel's main enemy during the reign of Saul and at the beginning of David's reign. It may come as a surprise, therefore, to learn that some of David's most loyal supporters were Philistines. According to 1 Samuel 27, Saul's insane jealousy and relentless pursuit of David forced him to seek asylum with Saul's enemies, the Philistines. Specifically, David went to the Philistine city of Gath and sought help from its king, Achish (27:1–4). Much later, after David had been king over Israel for several years, his son Absalom led a revolt against him (2 Sam. 15:1–12). A large percentage of Israelites joined the revolt, forcing David to flee Jerusalem (15:13–17). As he fled, the first group of supporters to join him were his royal bodyguard, called "the Cherethites and Pelethites." These, the most faithful of David's soldiers, were in fact Philistines who had followed him since his days in Gath (15:18), and together with their leader, Ittai, they swore to remain loyal to David to the death (15:21).

Two more brief examples of "foreigners" who became a part of Israel under David will suffice for our present purposes. After David's army had put down the revolt and Absalom was dead, two messengers volunteered to carry the tidings back to David (2 Sam. 18:19–33). One of them is called simply "Cushite." As we have seen, this is a reference to a person of African descent, and it indicates that there were black people living in ancient Israel and serving in David's army. Finally, a story in 2 Samuel 24 and 1 Chronicles 21 tells how David selected and purchased the plot of land where the Temple would be built in Jerusalem. He bought it from a man named Araunah (Ornan in Chronicles), who is called a Jebusite. The Jebusites were another of the peoples of Canaan listed in Deuteronomy 7:1, and the pre-Israelite inhabitants of Jerusalem, from whom David conquered the city according to 2 Samuel 5:6–10 (1 Chronicles 11:4–9). Araunah's continued presence there as a property owner suggests that little changed for the Jebusites when David took over. He did not kill them, enslave them, or confiscate their property. He simply annexed Jerusalem to his burgeoning empire. Since he made the city his capital, it would eventually change radically. But at the outset the Jebusites continued their lives as usual, only under David's government as residents of the new nation of Israel instead of as an autonomous Jebusite enclave. In all these examples the Bible indicates that Israel's ethnic diversity begun at the exodus continued under its kings so that the nation became something of a "melting pot" of originally different ethnic groups.

The Emergence of
Israel in History

At the beginning of this chapter I mentioned the evidence from history, including archaeology, as providing important background and balance for much of the Bible's record. One of the most perplexing and complicated issues faced by biblical scholars, archaeologists, and historians of ancient Israel in recent decades has been that of Israel's emergence as a people and a nation. It is fair to say that there is at present a growing consensus that Israel basically came from within Canaan. While outside influences, such as the "Moses group" from Egypt, may have helped to develop a national identity, by and large Israel was an indigenous development. In other words, in origin the Israelites *were* Canaanites, sharing a common ethnic background and culture. This picture accords with what the Bible says about Israel incorporating various ethnic, especially Canaanite, elements. Together, these stories furnish a forceful response to the texts surveyed in the preceding chapter, which use animosity toward non-Israelites as a way of trying to achieve a sense of national solidarity and religious "purity."

5

"Your People
Will Be My People"

The Story of Ruth

She was forty-five years old in 1955, a woman of quiet dignity who worked in a department store in downtown Montgomery, Alabama. But her quiet ways belied her strength. She was also secretary of the Montgomery NAACP. She rode the bus to and from work, and over the years had experienced difficulties with more than one bus driver for her defiance of the racist rules. Twelve years earlier she had been evicted from a bus for refusing to use the back door. On her way home on December 1, 1955, she sat in the only vacant seat, on the front row of the "black" section of the bus. Two stops later, the "white" seats were all occupied when a white man got on. The driver told the people at the front of the "black" seats to vacate the row. Three of the people on that row moved, but Rosa Parks was tired of being humiliated for racial reasons, and she stayed put. The driver threatened to have her arrested, and then made good on his threat. From the police station Mrs. Parks called E. D. Nixon, leader of the local NAACP. Early the next morning Mr. Nixon began calling people in town, especially ministers, to discuss plans for a boycott of the Montgomery bus system. Among those he called was the twenty-six-year-old minister of the Dexter Avenue Baptist Church, who had moved to Montgomery just a year earlier after the completion of his doctorate at Boston University. The young man's name was Martin Luther King Jr.

The story we will examine in this chapter is that of another courageous and dignified woman. Ruth exemplifies other positive qualities also, as we shall see. Her story may be read as a response to the laws about foreigners in Deuteronomy, particularly that of Deuteronomy 23:3: "No Ammonite or Moabite may enter the congregation of Yahweh."

A Genealogical Clue
(Matt. 1:1–17)

The Gospel of Matthew begins its account of Jesus' life with his genealogy. It is a heritage that any Jew of the time would have been proud to have. According to it, Jesus was of royal blood, boasting descent not only from Abraham but also from David. This is an important part of Matthew's overall message, which is directed to a Jewish or Jewish Christian audience. This fact may explain why Matthew's genealogy for Jesus differs so much from Luke's (Luke 3:23–38). Matthew's genealogy reminds his audience that Jesus was the "king of the Jews." Another title for the king was the Hebrew word "Messiah," which corresponds to the Greek word "Christ," both meaning "anointed." So Matthew is also making the point through his genealogy that Jesus is the anticipated Messiah or Christ.

Most of the genealogy for Jesus in Matthew comes straight out of the Old Testament, so that the names in it would have been familiar to its readers. Again, there would have been no finer pedigree among Jesus' Jewish contemporaries. But one feature of this genealogy may have stood out to Matthew's original audience—namely, the fact that it contains references to several women. A survey of other genealogies in the Bible shows that they usually are traced strictly through the male ancestors. Matthew mentions five women: Tamar (1:3), Rahab (1:5), Ruth (1:5), Bathsheba—called "the wife of Uriah" (1:7), and Mary (1:16). All these women, except of course Mary, are subjects of Old Testament stories. Each story brings out fascinating details about the women themselves and illuminating insights into the characters of the famous men who are involved with them. All five women were at least accused of sexual impropriety: Rahab, whom we have treated, was a prostitute; Ruth, as we shall see, appeared (at least) to seduce Boaz; Bathsheba was an adulteress; Mary was thought to have been unfaithful to Joseph (Matt. 1:18–19). Tamar's story (Genesis 38) is the most interesting in this regard. In the guise of a prostitute, she had sex with her father-in-law, Judah, and conceived twins by him. But the story makes it obvious that she was forced by his broken promises to take these actions in order to maintain her dignity as a woman in that culture. At the end of the story (v. 26) Judah acknowledges, "She is more righteous than I."

The inclusion of these women in Matthew's genealogy for Jesus makes a theological point. They bring to the reader's attention the real nature of Jesus' "illustrious" human roots. The women in the genealogy, like Tamar, are in fact victims of their male-dominated society, and specifically of the "great men" of the Old Testament who are involved with them. Tamar was abused by Judah. Rahab and Ruth show that the only options available to single women were prostitution and poverty. Bathsheba, according to 1 Samuel 11—12, was a passive party to the fulfillment of King David's lust. Matthew brings this out by not using her name, calling her instead "the wife of Uriah." Expanding from the women's stories to consider the entire genealogy, the reader recognizes that Israel's royal line was dominated by wicked men. Jesus' family history is a history of sin. But herein lies Matthew's theological lesson: the sinless one came among sinful humanity as one of them in order to redeem them before God.

A final observation about the women in Jesus' genealogy according to Matthew is especially germane to our study of racism. Three of the five women mentioned here—Tamar, Rahab, and Ruth—were non-Israelites. Tamar and Rahab were Canaanites, Ruth a Moabite. Again, there is a subtle point, particularly relevant for Matthew's original audience. The royal, Davidic line which Jesus represented was never "pure" Israelite or Jewish—all three of these women were in fact ancestors of David. Jesus represents and redeems all people. Moreover, these three "foreign" women are especially admirable characters for their intelligence, strength, and faithfulness. We have seen this with Rahab and touched on it with Tamar. Ruth's story remains, and she may be the best example of these qualities.

"Whither Thou Goest"
(Ruth 1)

The book of Ruth is a women's tale from start to finish. It is about women and told from a woman's perspective. The first five verses give background for the story. It is set in the time of the Judges, before the inception of the monarchy. A famine drives a family from Bethlehem to leave home and migrate across the Jordan to Moab. The man dies in Moab, leaving his wife, Naomi, and her two sons. Over the space of ten years the sons grow up and marry Moabite women. But then they, like their father, also die prematurely, so that Naomi is left alone with her daughters-in-law, Ruth and Orpah.

The three women share a close and affectionate relationship, so when Naomi decides to return to her native land, where the famine has abated (1:6), the other two determine initially to accompany her (1:7–10). In expressing her gratitude to them, Naomi lays out the theme for the book (1:8). She wishes for them the same *hesed* from Yahweh that they have shown to her. This word is variously translated as "faithfulness," "kindness," or "love." In the context of the book of Ruth it is probably best understood as "loving loyalty." Naomi's daughters-in-law have remained affectionately devoted to her throughout the ordeal of the loss of their male relatives. Now she wishes for them the same kind treatment from God.

Naomi demonstrates the genuineness of her feelings for her daughters-in-law by trying to persuade them to do what is in their own best interests. In a man's world, the only way they will be able to find "rest" or "security" again is by remarrying (1:9). And their chances of finding other husbands will be better among their own people. Naomi tells her daughters-in-law that with her they have no hope of security, since she is too old to have any more sons (1:11), and even if she could remarry and bear sons, they would have to wait until the sons were grown to marry them (1:12–13).

Naomi's speech persuades one of her daughters-in-law, Orpah, who decides to return to Moab. But Ruth stays. Naomi tries once more to get her to turn back. Ruth replies with a litany of pledges of her loyalty, which are well known to modern readers because of their frequent use in weddings:

> Do not press me to leave you,
> to turn back from behind you.

> For wherever you go I will go,
> wherever you lodge I will lodge.

> Your people will be my people,
> and your God my God.

Where you die I will die,
and there I will be buried.

So may Yahweh do to me and more—
only death will separate me from you.
(Ruth 1:16, 17)

Ruth's words really are an extraordinary expression of faithfulness to her mother-in-law. She is giving up everything she has known—her homeland and native culture, her family and people, even her religion—in order to accompany Naomi back to Bethlehem. Naomi does not make any more effort to persuade Ruth to stay behind, because her determination is plain (1:18).

When they reach Bethlehem, Naomi is recognized by former acquaintances there (1:19). She suggests, however, a name change for herself to reflect her personal experiences. "Don't call me Naomi anymore," she says. Naomi means "pleasant." Her new name, she says, should be Mara, meaning "bitter," for that has been her life's experience—God has dealt bitterly with her (1:20). She blames Yahweh for her problems. She does not explain why, only that she left full but has returned empty (1:21).

Meeting Boaz
(Ruth 2)

The book of Ruth is very intriguing theologically. Aside from the blame that Naomi imputes to Yahweh for her predicament, the book never ascribes any specific action to him. It speaks rather of an amazing set of coincidences. The first of these comes at the beginning of chapter 2, where Ruth, who has gone into the fields to glean what the reapers do not harvest on their first pass, just "happens" to end up in the field of Boaz, who "happens" to be a relative of Naomi's dead husband (2:1–3). Boaz also "happens" to be a wealthy nobleman (2:1). Of course, Ruth's actions in this episode are another testimony to her illustrious character. Not only is she loving and loyal to Naomi, but she is also industrious and generous. She expresses no self-pity; she does not bemoan her desperate situation. Rather, she takes the initiative to do what she can to better her circumstances and those of her mother-in-law. Perhaps it is her industry that first attracts Boaz's attention (2:5). At any rate, his servants point out what a hard worker Ruth is, noting that she has been in the field all day from early morning (2:7).

Boaz is quite impressed by Ruth's industry. He also is a person of good character. He is kind and generous to Ruth, taking her under his wing to make sure she is safe in the field (2:9). He also sees to it that she has water when she is thirsty (2:9) and food at mealtime (2:14). He even has his reapers leave a little extra behind to make her gleaning easier and more productive (2:16). But it is still her story, not his. Boaz's deeds of kindness are a sort of reward to Ruth, not only for her hard work, which he has witnessed, but also for what he has heard about Ruth. Her reputation as a loyal and devoted daughter-in-law has spread widely and become known to Boaz (2:11–12). Boaz recognizes the extraordinary unselfishness of Ruth's leaving her family and homeland for a foreign country, all out of love for Naomi (2:11).

All of this takes place before Ruth realizes that Boaz is a relative. It is not until the evening when she returns home from her first day in the field that Ruth discovers who Boaz is. She brings to Naomi the food she had left over from her meal as well as the grain she gleaned. It is an astonishing amount, about an ephah (in modern terms over half a bushel) of threshed barley (2:17)! When Ruth identifies Boaz as the man who was kind to her and in whose field she gleaned (2:19), Naomi recognizes him as a kinsman (2:20). She advises Ruth to accept Boaz's hospitality and remain with his harvesters for the remainder of the season (2:21–22), which she does (2:23).

A Night at the Threshing Floor (Ruth 3)

At the end of the harvest season Naomi concocts a plan to help Ruth secure a better future for herself. Boaz is now involved with threshing the grain that has been harvested. Naomi counsels Ruth to bathe herself and dress in her best clothing for a trip to the threshing floor, a flat area where the grain was separated out and piled (3:3). Ruth is to watch Boaz secretly until he has eaten and lies down to sleep. Then she is to "uncover his feet" (or "legs") and lie down until he directs her what to do (3:4).

It is not entirely certain what lies behind Naomi's instructions and Ruth's execution of them. This episode has clear sexual overtones, but it is hard to know how far Ruth's and Boaz's intimacy goes. The verb "to know" (3:3) is often used for sexual relations in the Bible, and the word "feet" is a relatively common euphemism for the genitals. So, is the entire expression "to uncover the feet" also idiomatic? That is, does Naomi tell Ruth to have sex with Boaz? Or does she intend for Ruth to expose Boaz's genitals so that he will think he has had sex with her and will "do the right thing" by marrying her? Or is the significance of Ruth's actions based on some other custom?

The laws in Deuteronomy provide some help for understanding the background of the story in Ruth, but they do not always apply exactly. Deuteronomy 24:19–22 gives laws about harvesting various agricultural products that are helpful for Ruth. A landowner is to have some of the produce left behind for the benefit of resident aliens, orphans, and *widows*. Deuteronomy 22:28–29 requires that a man who violates an unbetrothed virgin must marry her and may never divorce her. Some comparable practice may lie behind Naomi's instructions to Ruth, except that Ruth is a widow and not a virgin. Finally, Deuteronomy 25:5–10 describes the practice of levirate marriage, whereby the brother of a dead man is responsible for marrying his widow and fathering and raising a son to continue the dead brother's name. Again, some form of this practice is presupposed by the story in Ruth, but it is not exactly the same. Neither Boaz nor the nearer kinsman mentioned in 3:12 are brothers to Ruth's dead husband, yet each is called a "redeemer" (Hebrew *go'el*).

Whatever the relationship of the story to Israel's laws and customs, the interesting thing for our present study is that Ruth departs from Naomi's instructions in a telling way. She goes to the threshing floor and waits for Boaz (3:6). He arrives, having eaten and drunk (wine), so that his "heart is good," that is, he is content (3:7), but his head is probably not entirely clear. After he falls asleep Ruth "uncovers his feet" and lies down, as per Naomi's advice. Boaz awakens in the middle of the night and discovers a woman lying "at his feet." When he inquires as to her identity, Ruth's answer once more betrays her loyal concern for her mother-in-law: "I am Ruth, your maidservant. Spread your cloak [or "wing"] over your maidservant, for you are a redeemer." Her request that Boaz "spread his cloak" over her is a marriage proposal, and this is certainly in line with Naomi's plan. But Ruth's added note that he is a "redeemer" indicates that she has more on her mind than her own marriage. She is also concerned that Naomi will be cared for and that Naomi's husband's line will be continued. She, Ruth, will bear the heir that Naomi has lost. Ruth's unselfish love shines through.

In this episode, as in her gleaning, Ruth shows her strength of character. In both instances, she takes the initiative. It was she who entered the fields to gather food for Naomi and herself. Now, with Boaz, she again takes the leading role. It is she, not he, who proposes marriage and who thus forces the issue of the responsibility of the redeemer to care for the widow of a kinsman. Boaz is charmed by Ruth and blesses her for seeking him rather than a younger man (3:10). But he is also aware that there is a redeemer who is a closer blood relative than he. Ruth may have been aware of this herself, since she referred to Boaz as *a* redeemer rather than *the* redeemer (3:9). Nonetheless, her initiative, especially on behalf of her mother-in-law, has begun the process of providing for the widow according to the Israelite custom of levirate marriage. Ruth stays with Boaz at the threshing floor until just before dawn. Before she leaves he not only promises to take care of the matter of redemption but also gives her a quantity of barley to take to Naomi as a gift. Naomi's respect for and confidence in Boaz is apparent in her final statement to Ruth in this scene that he will not rest until he has settled the matter that very day (3:18).

In the Gate
(Ruth 4:1–12)

The final scene of the book of Ruth takes place in the city gate, which was the courtroom of ancient Israelite cities. It was the site where important legal and civic matters of cities were decided. Boaz brings the case of Naomi's redemption before ten elders of the city whom he has assembled (4:1–2). Again, it is providential that the kinsman who is a nearer redeemer shows up at the gate about the same time Boaz does, since this other man knows nothing of the affair. Boaz introduces a piece of information that is new to the story—Naomi owns a parcel of land that belonged to her husband, and she now wishes to sell it. How this could be is something of a mystery in the story, since Naomi and Ruth have appeared to be penniless heretofore. It is possible that Naomi did not know of the land or that she assumed it was lost because of her long absence. It may have been taken over by squatters, as in the story of the Shunammite woman's land in 2 Kings 8:1–6. At any rate, Boaz presents the case as a matter of land to be redeemed, bought back into the family heritage (4:4).

When the nearer kinsman expresses his willingness to buy the land, Boaz introduces another element—the redeemer's responsibility entails marrying Ruth and fathering children by her so that the line of her husband will continue (4:5). This new condition means that the nearer kinsman must decline to be the redeemer. He says it would damage his own inheritance (4:6), by which he probably means the inheritance for his own children. If buying the land were the only thing involved, he could profit from its produce and recover his investment by selling it later. But with Ruth in the equation, it would mean having to care for her and Naomi as well as any children Ruth would bear. It would also mean that the land and its produce would go to Ruth's son. Thus, the man would not recover his investment and would in fact diminish the inheritance he will leave to his other children.

Boaz is next in line to redeem. He has followed the accepted procedure in front of witnesses, so that he cannot be accused of any underhanded dealing. He acquires Naomi's land, and it is clear that for him this entails caring for her (4:9). He also acquires Ruth as his wife, with the understanding that he will raise children to maintain the name of her former husband (4:10). Boaz is apparently single or widowed and without children. He is wealthy, and no other heir of his is mentioned. According to the custom of the day, a sandal is exchanged between Boaz and the other relative to seal the arrangement (4:7). The elders bless Ruth by the ancestral mothers of Israel, Rachel and Leah (4:11), and by the ancestors of the tribe of Judah—Perez, Tamar, and Judah himself (4:12). Ruth is fully welcomed and integrated into the nation of Israel, the tribe of Judah, the city of Bethlehem, and the clan of Boaz.

A Genealogical Conclusion
(Ruth 4:13–22)

From the standpoint of Ruth and especially of Naomi, the story ends at the other extreme from where it began. Naomi, who referred to herself as empty and bitter at the beginning, is now full and happy. This is because Ruth bears a son, Obed, to continue Naomi's line. Indeed, Naomi is treated as the child's mother. She nurses him (4:16), and the neighbor women refer to him as her son (4:17). These women observe that Naomi is blessed to have a redeemer in Boaz (4:14), who has "restored" Naomi by begetting a son for her and who will take care of her in her old age (4:15). But most of all they take note of Naomi's good fortune in having a daughter-in-law like Ruth, who loves her and is more valuable to her than seven sons (4:15). Thanks to Ruth, Naomi becomes the ancestress of Israel's greatest king, David (4:17). Nevertheless, the book ends in an irony. The genealogy of David in 4:18–22, which may be a later addition to the book, traces his ancestry through Boaz, just as the one in Matthew does, rather than through Naomi's husband or son. Perhaps it is only just that Ruth, who gave up so much for her mother-in-law, should in the final analysis receive the honor she deserves as the real great-grandmother of David, despite her origins as a foreigner, a Moabite.

part three

Who Are God's People?

6

"You Shall Have No Part with Us"

Mixed Marriages in Ezra-Nehemiah

My wife is from Panama—not the Canal Zone, but the actual Latin-American country—so I know something about intercultural and interethnic marriages. We were married in Panama and lived there during our first year together. Because of its narrow span between the Atlantic and Pacific Oceans, the country has been a global crossroads since the New World was discovered, and even more so in this century, with the canal. Various native tribes were there in the sixteenth century when the Europeans, especially the Spanish, began to arrive. Black people from both Africa and the Caribbean and Asians, especially Chinese, came later to work on the canal. Panamanian society is well integrated, and interracial marriage is common. During the time we lived there, I got to know a man named Jones who worked on small construction projects and maintenance around the seminary where I was teaching. I never knew his first name; everyone just called him Brother Jones. He was in his sixties and retired. Originally from the States, he had lived in Panama over thirty years. He had settled there after World War II with his wife, a woman of Jamaican extraction. He was white; she was black. In the United States their marriage had been rejected by his family and was, in fact, illegal in his home state shortly after the war. So they had moved to Panama, where they were freely accepted.

In this chapter, we will examine another movement toward exclusivism from within ancient Israel. Actually, it is a continuation of the theme we explored in chapter 3, since its leaders,

Ezra and Nehemiah, cite the laws about the Canaanites in Deuteronomy as their authority. The specific matter at issue is marriage between Jews and non-Jews.

Background and Setting

As has been mentioned, the Deuteronomistic History recounts a series of crucial events that shaped the nations of Israel and Judah. The first of these was the division of the united kingdom, which had been ruled by Saul, David, and Solomon, into the separate countries of Israel and Judah. This took place after the death of Solomon in about 922 B.C. and was caused by his idolatry, according to 1 Kings 11. The heirs of David and Solomon, who made up the Davidic dynasty, continued to reign in Judah, while Israel went through a series of royal houses established by army generals who revolted against their kings. Israel as a separate nation came to an end in 721 B.C. when its capital, Samaria, was demolished by the Assyrian army. A significant portion of the population was deported to other parts of the Assyrian empire, and foreigners were brought in to settle what had been Israel. The Deuteronomistic author(s) again explained this event as punishment for the sin, especially idolatry, of the people of Israel (2 Kings 17). Eventually Judah also fell prey to a foreign power. Second Kings 25 recounts how its capital, Jerusalem, was destroyed by the Babylonians in 586 B.C. and most of its inhabitants were taken into exile to Babylon—once more the result of sin.

The Deuteronomistic History and its theology had an enormous impact on Old Testament thought and literature during the Babylonian exile and beyond. We will see in this chapter that some leaders and writers gave a narrow interpretation to the regulations of Deuteronomy concerning other peoples. But we will also see here and in future chapters that other writers responded with more openness, and that some of those writers were themselves non-Israelites.

Return and Conflict

In 539 B.C. the Babylonian empire was conquered by the Persians, whose policies toward conquered peoples differed from those of the Babylonians. The new Persian king, Cyrus, allowed people from Judah to return home beginning in 538. Because of this, the book of Isaiah even refers to Cyrus as Yahweh's "shepherd" (44:28) and Messiah ("anointed," 45:1)! The books of Chronicles and of Ezra-Nehemiah end and begin, respectively, with the edict of Cyrus permitting the people of Judah to go home and rebuild the Temple (2 Chron. 36:22–23; Ezra 1:1–4). This was the first of several waves of returnees. Unfortunately, little is known of this first group. Their leader may have been the Sheshbazzar named in Ezra 1:5–11. They apparently set about reconstructing the Temple, but were unable to do any more than lay its foundations (Ezra 5:16).

A few years later, a second group arrived under the dual leadership of Zerubbabel and Jeshua (Ezra 3:2). Encouraged by the prophets Haggai and Zechariah (Ezra 5:1–2), this group succeeded in completing the Temple in the space of the five years between 520 and 515 B.C. The success of these builders came in the face of strong local opposition, which may have been a factor in the failure of Sheshbazzar and which would resurface in the later missions of Nehemiah and Ezra. According to Ezra 4:1–5, when the returnees from Judah first began to rebuild, the "people of the land" (v. 4) offered to help but were rebuffed. The reasons were ethnic and religious. These "people of the land" were the heirs of those who had been resettled there by the Assyrians after 721 B.C. (Ezra 4:2, 9–10). They considered themselves worshipers of Yahweh just like those returning from Babylon (4:2). But Zerubbabel and those with him had a very different point of view: "You shall have no part with us in building a temple to our God" (4:3). They regarded the inhabitants of Samaria as a mongrel race, the result of the mixing of Israelites who had been left behind by the Assyrians with the foreign peoples who had been imported or had squatted on the vacant land. This is essentially the Deuteronomistic perspective of 2 Kings 17. The returnees under Zerubbabel also considered these local inhabitants to be religious apostates who had abandoned the worship of Yahweh or diluted and perverted it with influences from foreign religions. All of this was the beginning of the Jewish-Samaritan conflict that we will encounter in the New Testament. In short, Zerubbabel and Jeshua saw their mission as establishing a colony of pure Israelites or Jews, ethnically and religiously, in the city that they viewed as their national and religious heritage. Their successors, Nehemiah and Ezra, would adopt much the same viewpoint.

Ezra and Nehemiah

At different points within the next century and a quarter Ezra and Nehemiah each came to Jerusalem. Nehemiah made two visits and supervised the reconstruction of Jerusalem's city wall. The books in the Bible that bear their names were originally a single volume. Over the years, however, different portions of it have gotten out of order. As a result, the dates and historical details of the visits of both Ezra and Nehemiah are uncertain. It is not even entirely clear which of them came first. Both were especially concerned, like their predecessors, with reinstituting the purity of the Jewish community in Jerusalem and its worship of Yahweh. Also like their predecessors, both encountered significant opposition from some of the local inhabitants. The reasons were varied, but a principal one was political. The Samaritan officials who controlled Jerusalem saw the newcomers as outsiders and invaders who threatened to diminish their power (Neh. 4:1–2 [3:33–34 Heb.]). Both groups were vying for the favor of the Persian authorities, as the exchange of letters with the Persian court in Ezra 4—6 shows. But for Ezra and Nehemiah, the controversy was fundamentally ethnic, national, and religious. Like Zerubbabel and Jeshua, they considered the Samaritans to be a mongrel race of religious apostates, whose very existence was a threat to the ethnic and religious purity that they sought to (re)establish.

It is this desire for purity, ethnically and religiously defined, that leads both Ezra and Nehemiah to a strict and harsh interpretation of Deuteronomy's injunction against foreign marriages. Both consider it a serious crisis and offense that some of the Jews have married foreign women (Ezra 9—10; Neh. 13:23–27). However, it is striking that the definition of prohibited marriages has changed. Both Ezra and Nehemiah cite Deuteronomy 7 as their authority (Ezra 9:11–12; Neh. 13:25). But while this passage forbids marriages with the indigenous Canaanite groups, the prohibition in Ezra and Nehemiah has expanded to include all non-Israelites. Nehemiah 13:23 does not mention any Canaanite tribes at all, but only women of Ashdod (Philistines), Ammon, and Moab. Ezra 9:1 mentions not only Canaanites, Hittites, Perizzites, and Jebusites, but also Ammonites, Moabites, Egyptians, and Amorites. Boaz's marriage to Ruth would have been forbidden under this interpretation! Moreover, Ezra 10:2 refers to women from "the peoples of the land," which is nearly the same expression as the one in 4:4 referring to the Samaritans. Thus, the prohibition in Deuteronomy, which was limited to the native Canaanites and was specifically because of their religious practices, is interpreted in Ezra and Nehemiah to include all non-Jews, apparently even those whose ancestors included members of the former kingdom of Israel.

Ezra's solution to the problem is not much less harsh than that envisioned by Deuteronomy, and is driven by the same sense of need to define and consolidate the nation in the face of calamity. Ezra compels those with him to "put away" their non-Jewish wives, along with their children. This means, of course, divorce, but its consequences would have been far more severe at that time than today. As suggested in earlier chapters, an unmarried woman in that society had few means of support. If she could not remarry (and a divorced woman would have been regarded to a certain extent as "damaged goods") or find a male relative (usually father or brother) to live with, her options were basically prostitution or begging. The children of these marriages would have been fatherless and homeless, with no roots within a clan or family and no hope of any inheritance. Nehemiah does not specifically mention divorce, though it seems likely that this would have been his solution as well, especially in light of his summary claim in 13:30: "I cleansed them from everything foreign."

Contemporary Responses

In the following chapters we will explore the universalism of the book of Jonah and of wisdom literature in the Old Testament as responses to the narrowness of Ezra-Nehemiah. Before ending this chapter, however, it will be useful to mention two biblical books roughly contemporary with Ezra-Nehemiah that seem to differ in their stances on the Samaritans and on "mixed" marriages and may indeed be responding directly to Ezra-Nehemiah about these matters.

Who Are God's People?

The Chronicler's "All Israel"

The books of 1 and 2 Chronicles are roughly contemporary with Ezra-Nehemiah. The exact date is debated, but is is clear that these books as we now have them in the Bible have undergone at least one level of editing in common. For many years, in fact, Chronicles-Ezra-Nehemiah were all considered the work of a single individual. That view has been disputed in recent decades, partly on the basis of differences in outlook between 1 and 2 Chronicles on the one hand and Ezra-Nehemiah on the other. One of these crucial differences concerns the attitude toward the people in what had been the northern kingdom of Israel. We have seen that Ezra-Nehemiah rejected these Samaritans as illegitimate, both ethnically and religiously. They refused to have anything to do with the Samaritans and condemned intermarriage with them.

Now, the book of 2 Chronicle tells the story of the kingdom of Judah, following the Deuteronomistic account in 1 and 2 Kings fairly closely. One major difference, however, is that 2 Chronicles leaves out any reference to the northern kingdom of Israel except for those episodes in which Israel is involved with Judah. This glaring omission was taken for a long time as an indication that the author, the "Chronicler," shared Ezra-Nehemiah's disdain for the Israelite remnant, the Samaritans. There are certainly indications that the Chronicler regarded the Israelites as apostates. This seems clear from the speech of Abijah, king of Judah, to King Jeroboam and the Israelites in 2 Chronicles 13:4–12. But the Chronicler does not treat Israel as a lost cause. The book of 1 Chronicles (chaps. 1—9) begins with a list of genealogies, not just of Judah, but of all the tribes of Israel. And throughout 1 Chronicles especially there are references to "all Israel" acting and working together in the ideal age under David and Solomon. In 2 Chronicles (30:1–2), Hezekiah is commended for inviting people from Israel (here called Ephraim and Manasseh) to keep the Passover in Jerusalem, and Josiah (34:6–7, 33) for carrying out religious reforms in the north. Even in Abijah's speech, the intent seems to be to entice the people of Israel back to the proper worship of God in the Temple (13:10–11). In other words, the Chronicler does not simply reject the Samaritans and refuse to have anything to do with them, as do Ezra and Nehemiah. Quite the contrary, the Chronicler sees them still as part of God's people,

Israel. They have gone astray, but the Chronicler calls them back and gives every indication of wanting to welcome them back to the restoration of proper religous practice in the Jerusalem temple.

Marriage and Divorce
in Malachi 2:10–16

The prophet Malachi was another contemporary, roughly speaking, of Ezra and Nehemiah. Nothing is known of him outside of this book. It is not even clear whether "Malachi," which means "my messenger," was the author's real name or is simply a title. The idea of covenant faithfulness is central to the book, and one kind of covenant that Malachi discusses is marriage. The passage where this discussion occurs, 2:10–16, is difficult to interpret. It accuses the people of Judah of profaning two covenants—the "covenant of our ancestors" (2:10) and the covenant of marriage (2:14). They have profaned the first covenant by "marrying the daughter of a foreign god" (2:11). This accusation refers to marriage with foreign women, as in Ezra-Nehemiah, or perhaps to idolatry. In either case, the expression "daughter of a foreign god" indicates that the offense is, in the author's view, religious in nature rather than ethnic. Indeed, the writer's appeal to creation in verse 10 would tend to undercut the use of this text against any ethnic group. Here there are two rhetorical questions: "We all have one father, do we not? One God has created us, has he not?" The author may mean Jews when he says "we" and "us" (note the reference to "divine offspring" in 2:15). However, our treatment of Genesis 1—3 in chapter 1 showed that creation attests the unity and equality of all people in God's eyes.

The condemnation of divorce in verses 14–16 may be in direct response to the campaign of Ezra-Nehemiah for Jews to "put away" their "foreign" wives. This would be especially likely if 2:10–12 is directed against idolatry. But even if 2:10–12 is against foreign marriages, like Ezra-Nehemiah, their point is undercut by the subsequent oracle against divorce. After all, even marriage with a foreign woman is a covenant (v. 14). Thus, the principles of the text in Malachi 2:10–16 counter the call in Ezra-Nehemiah to put away foreign wives and children, and Malachi 2:14–16 may be a direct rebuttal of this aspect of Ezra's and Nehemiah's missions.

7

"The Ear That Hears and the Eye That Sees"

The Non-Israelite Origins of Wisdom in Israel

My older daughter was just starting school when I moved to Memphis in 1983. I was astounded at the large number of parochial schools in the city. It seemed that each church had its own "Christian academy." I was informed that this was a legacy of reaction to desegregation a generation earlier. When black students were bused in to formerly "white" public schools, many white parents withdrew their children. Academies sprang up in white churches throughout the South to accommodate them. A further result of this phenomenon was the effective impoverishment of the city school system, since those without children in the public schools generally opposed measures to raise money for them.

Recently, I heard a teacher in one of the city's oldest and poorest elementary schools appeal for contributions to buy Christmas presents for the children in her class. She described the generally dismal conditions of her classroom—the deterioration of the building and the nearly unbearable heat and odors on the sweltering days at the beginning and end of the school year. She touched on the violence that these inner city children experience, how it is common for some of them to go to sleep to the sound of gunfire. But what moved me most, perhaps because that day was my daughter's birthday, was when she explained that the present she gave them would be the only one some of them had ever received. At the beginning of the year, she said, when she filled out forms for each student in her class, she would ask for each child's birthday. Often she had received the reply, "I ain't got one. My momma never tol' me 'bout dat."

Wisdom, which we discuss in this chapter, was a kind of ancient philosophy and educational system. The presence of wisdom thought and literature in Israel provides a kind of response to the exclusiveness of movements such as those of Ezra and Nehemiah, because wisdom was an international phenomenon, one based not on any specific religious tradition, but on observation of the natural world.

The Nature of Wisdom

The portions of the Bible that we have discussed so far all have in common that they were written by Israelites. Even Ruth's story is not in her own words. But there are important parts of the Bible that were written by non-Israelites. The best examples are in those books that represent what is known as wisdom literature.

"Wisdom" designates both a type of literature and an approach to life that are reflected in the biblical books of Job, Proverbs, and Ecclesiastes (also known as Qoheleth). It was a kind of ancient philosophy or contemplation about the nature and meaning of life. Its judgments and conclusions are based not on history or special revelation, as is the rest of the Bible, but on observation of and reasoning about the world and its workings. Thus, wisdom finds its source of information and inspiration in creation:

> The ear that hears and the eye that sees—
> Yahweh made them both.
>
> (Prov. 20:12)

The advice it gives is usually quite practical and sometimes "secular," since in part it is a "common sense" approach to life based on day-to-day experience:

> Let your foot be seldom in your neighbor's house
> lest he grow tired of you and hate you.
>
> (Prov. 25:17)

> Do not be overly righteous or too wise;
> Why should you destroy yourself?
> > (Eccl. 7:16)

But wisdom is never far from matters of religion. It also makes observations about God and God's involvement in the world. It sees the everyday, surrounding world as a revelation of God and hence presents a kind of "natural theology."

> One who oppresses a poor person insults his Maker,
> but one who is kind to the needy honors him.
> > (Prov. 14:31)

Since it was based on observation of the natural world, wisdom in ancient Israel was not limited to any one social stratum. Just as with modern aphorisms ("Nothing ventured, nothing gained," "What goes around comes around," "No time like the present"), most of the short one- or two-line "proverbs" in the Bible probably arose among common people, garnered from their everyday experiences.

> The glory of youths is their strength,
> but the beauty of the aged is their gray hair.
> > (Prov. 20:29)

> A living dog is better than a dead lion.
> > (Eccl. 9:4)

But wisdom eventually became the special property of an elite class of scribes who were the educators in ancient Israel. They are called "the wise" in Prov. 24:23. The book of Proverbs, especially its first nine chapters, states repeatedly that its objective is instruction.

> My son, forget not my teaching,
> but let your heart preserve my commandments.
> > (Prov. 3:1)

> Now, sons, listen to me.
> Pay attention to the words of my mouth.
> > (Prov. 7:24)

The objects of this instruction, as these verses indicate, were specifically young males who were probably of the noble class.[5] They were the only ones who had the leisure to pursue education. This may explain why wisdom is so strongly associated in the Bible with royal courts. The various collections in Proverbs illustrate this well: Book I—"The proverbs of Solomon, the son of David, the king of Israel" (1:1); Book II—"The proverbs of Solomon" (10:1); Book IV—"These also are the proverbs of Solomon which the men of Hezekiah, the king of Judah, copied" (25:1); and the final chapter—"The words of Lemuel, the king of Massa, which his mother taught him" (31:1).

For our present puposes, it is especially interesting that Lemuel is not an Israelite. Massa was probably an area in northwestern Arabia. Proverbs 30 is also attributed to someone from Massa, though he is not designated as a king: "The words of Agur, the son of Jakeh of Massa."[6] Wisdom, in fact, was not the property of Israel, but was an international phenomenon, especially well attested in Egypt and Mesopotamia. In addition to chapters 30—31, Book III of Proverbs (22:17–24:22) is very similar to a wisdom document from ancient Egypt known as the Instruction of Amenemope and must have borrowed from it. Also, the story in the book of Job is similar to one of the earliest tales preserved from Mesopotamia. It is no coincidence that the Bible in 1 Kings 3—11 ascribes both great wisdom and extensive international contacts to Solomon. The emphasis of wisdom on natural revelation and its practical, common-sense approach explains why it could originate and develop in any country. Of course, the instances of wisdom literature in the Bible do refer frequently to Yahweh. But this is because they have adapted wisdom thought to Israel. There is nothing inherently Israelite or Yahwistic about wisdom. One might say that wisdom is God's gift and revelation for all people.

Proverbs

"Listen, My Son" (Chapters 1—9)

The use of wisdom to educate is nowhere clearer than in Proverbs 1—9. The audience is young noblemen, as indicated by the references to "my son" as well as the subject matter. The text constantly warns the young man to stay away from the "strange woman" (2:16–19; 5:1–6; 6:20–35; 7:1–27), who is characterized as an adulteress (2:17; 6:26; 7:19). Two things about this repeated warning are important for this study. First, the reasons given for which she should be avoided are eminently practical. Writers of other biblical books might appeal to the divinely revealed prohibition, "Thou shalt not commit adultery." But the writer of Proverbs instead warns of common-sense dangers: disease ("You will groan at your end when your skin and flesh are consumed," 5:11) and a husband's jealousy ("For jealousy is a man's rage. He will not spare when he takes revenge," 6:34). So when the writer says, "Her house is the paths of Sheol, descending to the chambers of death," the reference is not to some kind of spiritual punishment but to physical death, pure and simple.

Second, the exact meaning of the expression "strange woman" is "foreign woman." It probably should be understood idiomatically as a reference to a "loose woman" or "another woman," rather than as a reference to a non-Israelite. Proverbs 1—9 characterizes the faults of this type of woman as moral rather than ethnic. If the expression is taken literally as referring to "foreign" women, its argument is undercut by the basic principle of wisdom that revelation from God is in the created nature of the world and is available for all people to observe. It is also undercut by the fact that, by its own admission, much of Proverbs comes from non-Israelite authors and documents.

The contrast to the "strange woman," the one whom the wise man will pursue, is Wisdom herself. In Proverbs 8, Wisdom is personified as a woman who, like the "strange woman," seeks to entice men to follow her. The difference is that her way leads to prosperity (8:18). In the second half of chapter 8 Wisdom is given a very high place in the created order. She is the first of creation (8:22) and Yahweh's companion through the process of creating the universe (8:27–30). This passage illustrates our characterization of wisdom as the fundamental principle of the universe. But the lovely image of that principle essentially as God's wife, using erotically suggestive imagery, is very striking indeed and may well be borrowed from outside of Israel.

The Instruction of Amenemope and Proverbs 22:17–24:22

This section of Proverbs, which is often referred to as Book III, bears striking resemblance to the Egyptian "Instruction of Amenemope." The latter has thirty paragraphs, which explains the reference in Proverbs 22:20 to thirty sayings, although only ten or eleven of them are reproduced in Proverbs. This makes clear that it is the Bible that has borrowed from Amenemope and not the other way around, since the "thirty sayings" of Proverbs cannot otherwise be accounted for.

The Egyptian work has been adapted to its new Israelite setting, for there are three mentions of Yahweh in this section (22:19, 23; 23:17). The references to God as the strong Redeemer of the underprivileged (23:10) who weighs the heart of all people (24:12) call to mind the scenes of final judgment in the Egyptian Book of the Dead, in which an individual's heart is weighed against the feather of truth. Concern for social justice is one of the distinctive themes that Amenemope and Proverbs have in common. In this line, the injunction against moving a landmark appears twice (22:28; 23:10) as a safeguard against depriving poor farmers of their heritage and means of sustenance. But most of the advice in both documents is secular and common sense in nature, rather than theological. They also share an extended admonition against drunkenness as causing suffering (Prov. 23:29–35) and eventually financial ruin (23:19–21).

The Wise of Massa
(Proverbs 30–31)

The last two chapters of Proverbs are by foreign authors from Massa, probably in northwest Arabia (see note 6). The sayings of Agur in chapter 30 illustrate several typical features of wisdom. The argument for the existence of God in verse 4 is drawn from creation and presented as a series of rhetorical questions about God's role as maker and maintainer of the world. Although verses 1–14 contain a debate about God's existence, Yahweh's name is mentioned only once—in verse 9. The numerical proverbs beginning in verse 15 are based mainly on the natural world and its animal inhabitants—eagle and serpent (v. 19), ants, badgers, locusts, and lizards (vv. 24–28), and lion, rooster, and goat (vv. 30–31). They are common-sense observations without any theological content.

The teachings that Lemuel, king of Massa, received from his mother in Proverbs 31 are dominated by the description of the perfect or "good" wife in verses 10–31 and can therefore be read as a forceful response to any document against marrying non-Israelites. The text praises virtues such as efficiency and industry but says nothing about ethnicity. Only the mention of Yahweh in verse 30 connects it specifically with Israel. The instruction in verses 1–9 consists of three kinds of admonitions that are fitting for young nobles, especially the crown prince: Do not squander resources on women (v. 3), avoid (excessive) drinking (vv. 4–7), and judge fairly, maintaining the rights of the poor and disadvantaged (vv. 8–9). Again, the advice in these admonitions is practical and rational rather than theological in nature. The only reference to God in the chapter is verse 30's remark that a woman who fears Yahweh deserves praise.

Job

The book of Job is essentially a debate on the question of human suffering: Why do bad things happen to good people? The question is a perennial one as it touches on the very heart of what it means to be human. The basic story is a very old one. A version of it is among the most ancient writings from Mesopotamia. The biblical story may have been borrowed from Mesopotamia, although the issues it deals with are so universal that the plot and the various positions in the debate could have arisen independently. It is set in the land of Uz, which is probably Edom in southeastern Palestine (the southern area of modern-day Jordan). So Job was not Israelite.

The old story behind the book is preserved by and large in the prologue (chaps. 1—2) and epilogue (42:7–17), which are in prose. In this story, the question at issue was not so much the reason for suffering but rather why a person should serve God (note the question in 1:9: "Does Job fear God for nought?"). Job's sufferings were a test of his faithfulness, and his response was exemplary: "In all this Job did not sin or charge God with wrong" (1:22); "In all this Job did not sin with his lips" (2:10). The nature of the test inspired a later writer to make suffering the new focus of the work. This was accomplished by inserting the poetic dialogues between Job and his friends as a debate on the matter.

In the debate, Job's three friends, Eliphaz, Bildad, and Zophar, defend the orthodox position. They assume the principle that sin brings suffering and that righteousness brings prosperity. They assume, further, that the reverse is true—that all suffering must be punishment for sin and all prosperity reward for righteousness. They conclude, therefore, that Job's sufferings are deserved—punishment for sins that he must have committed in the past. Thus, Eliphaz in his opening speech asks Job,

> Who that was innocent ever perished?
> Where were the upright ever destroyed?
> (4:7)

Job also seems to accept these assumptions. The difference is that he knows he has not sinned, so he accuses God of injustice, of afflicting him without cause. He demands a face-to-face encounter with God so that he can make his case and have God answer his accusations:

> I would speak to Shaddai ["the Almighty"]
> I desire to dispute with God.
> (13:3)

He also accuses his three companions of lying for God:

> Indeed, you are whitewashers of a lie . . . .
> Will you speak falsely for God?
> Will you speak deceitfully for him?
> (13:4, 7)

The book obviously sides with Job. In chapters 38—42 God appears to him and questions him about creation. It is clear that Job is no match for God. Human beings cannot comprehend how the universe operates, much less direct it. God has purposes in Job's suffering that he cannot grasp. But at the same time, Job understands God better than his three friends do. Yahweh appears to Eliphaz and announces his anger against the three "because you have not spoken of me rightly like my servant Job."

The book of Job is a response to Deuteronomistic theology. The position of Job's friends that calamity is punishment for sin is very close to if not identical with the viewpoint of the Deuteronomistic History, which explains the destruction of Jerusalem as punishment for the sins of its inhabitants. But Job calls this simple equation into question; God is not bound by "orthodox" principles. The reasons for suffering are too complicated to be reduced to any kind of universal formula. The book's message is that God is worthy of trust even when humans do not understand what lies behind their troubles. If Job rebuffs the orthodox explanation of suffering, it also takes a more positive view of non-Israelites than the one that was current under Ezra and Nehemiah at the end of the exile. Job is called the most blameless and upright person on the earth (1:8), despite the fact that he is not an Israelite. The debate between him and his companions is based not on the law of Moses, but on their own experiences. Their standard, orthodox answers to questions such as the meaning of suffering are judged unacceptable because they are guilty of trying to make God in their own image and to hedge God about with their own set of rules. The nature and spirit of Job plead against the narrowness of prejudice.

Ecclesiastes

If Job questions orthodox views, the book of Ecclesiastes does so even more. It shares with all wisdom literature the contemplation of universal issues on the basis of reflection on experience and the created order.

> There is nothing better for mortals than to eat and drink and find enjoyment in their toil. (2:24a, NRSV)

A second voice has glossed the remarks of the first "speaker" with comments of a more pious or orthodox nature.

> This also I saw is from God's hand, for who can eat or feel pleasure apart from him? (2:24b–25)

The conclusion of the book especially reflects the latter perspective:

> The end of the matter. All is heard. Fear God and keep his commandments, for this is a person's whole duty. For God will bring every deed into judgment because of every secret thing, whether good or evil. (12:13–14)

The book of Ecclesiastes does not deal directly with issues of ethnicity. Rather, like all wisdom, it is contemplation that is universal in nature, not restricted by ethnic differences or national boundaries. It deals with concerns that all people have in common. Its ground of authority is creation, in which all people are equal before God.

8

"I Knew That You Are a Merciful God"

The Book of Jonah

Churches were at the heart of the civil rights movement of the 1960s. Dr. Martin Luther King Jr. and many other leaders of the movement were ministers. Predominantly white churches each have their own history of response to the times. What happened in one Memphis church was typical of many southern churches across denominations. This was a congregation of several hundred members near a university. The church had never had black members or considered any for membership. The issue had simply never arisen. Then, in the 1960s a black student began attending services. He was an African convert of missionaries from the denomination who had come to the States to study. Eventually, the man expressed a desire to join the church. The minister determined that the man's credentials were impeccable and that race should be no impediment. The leadership of the church agreed and designated a particular Sunday for the man to present himself for membership. Word of the plan spread like the proverbial wildfire throughout the membership of the church, so that on the Sunday in question the sanctuary was packed. He seized on the occasion to preach about all people being God's children and to ask how Christians could discriminate if God did not. The sermon did not change any minds, though it may have augmented the tension in the assembly. Finally, the moment everyone had been awaiting arrived. The minister concluded his sermon and offered an invitation to membership in the church. The black man came forward.

The minister took another five minutes trying to address the controversy of the situation and to explain the reasons behind his and the church leaders' decision. When he finally announced that the black man was welcome, about half of the congregation arose and left the building, never to return. This single event more than any other determined the direction of that church. Overnight, it became a small church, never regaining the numbers it had before that Sunday. Openness and tolerance became the guiding principles in subsequent policy decisions. Its positions more than once attracted the attention of the local media, so that today its voice on community matters belies its size.

The story of Jonah, which we treat in this chapter, was intended as a ludicrous antitype of a biblical prophet and perhaps of Israel as a nation, in order to show the ridiculous extremes to which nationalism and bigotry can drive a person. Jonah was a representative for God who chose to try to run from God rather than to fulfill his responsibility as God's spokesman. But the people who left the Memphis church—who sang hymns about spreading the gospel and gave money to support missionaries and then walked out when a black man joined—they show that Jonah's tale, however ludicrous it may seem, is not so far removed from reality.

Jonah

The story of Jonah's being swallowed by a large fish (the Bible does not actually call it a whale) is well known. Unfortunately, the message of the book of Jonah is often lost in the debate over whether the story actually happened. But the book is not really about a big fish or Jonah's endurance or even about a miracle from God. It is about prejudice and nationalism and God's universal love.

Jonah is unique among all the prophetic books of the Bible because it does not contain a collection of prophetic sermons or oracles. There is only one, very brief and direct oracle in the book: "Forty days more, and Nineveh will be overthrown" (Jonah 3:4). In another sense, though, the entire book is a sermon. A better word might be "parody." The character of Jonah is a parody—a satirical imitation of a real prophet, an exaggeration of distasteful qualities for the purpose of teaching a lesson.

This is another feature that makes Jonah unique. Unlike other prophets, who are admired for their courage and forthrightness, there is nothing admirable about Jonah.

The prophet Jonah is mentioned just once outside the book that bears his name (2 Kings 14:25). This Jonah lived and worked in eighth-century Israel under King Jeroboam II (ca. 786–746 B.C.). The book of Jonah itself was likely written at least three centuries later, when its author and audience remembered the Assyrians as the hated foreigners who had captured and destroyed the nation of Israel in 721 B.C. Jonah was probably chosen as the subject for the parody because his setting in the eighth century in the shadow of the great Assyrian empire, headquartered at Nineveh, made him a perfect candidate to teach a lesson about prejudice and nationalism. There may also be another reason why Jonah was chosen. His name means "dove," which is sometimes a symbol for Israel in the Bible (see Hos. 7:11). Thus, the target of the parody is not prophets but an attitude among some of the people of Israel. It is their ultranationalism and hateful prejudice toward other people that the writer wishes to counter. Jonah may even have been written in direct response to the narrow nationalistic movement of Ezra and Nehemiah. But whenever Jonah was written and whatever its historical value, it is the message of the book against prejudice and advocating the love of God for all people that speaks most forcefully to a modern audience.

The book of Jonah may also be seen as a drama. It divides neatly into three acts, with two scenes in the final act, and this is the structure we shall follow in discussing it.

Act One (1:1–16)

Throughout the book, Jonah is depicted as a ludicrous character whose understanding of God is obscured and corrupted by his nationalistic narrowness. The non-Israelites who are unfamiliar with Israel's God, Yahweh, actually display a better comprehension of who Yahweh is than does Yahweh's own prophet, Jonah. Nowhere is this clearer than in the first act.

The first three verses (1:1–3) set the stage for the first act. Jonah is commanded by Yahweh to go to Nineveh. "The word of Yahweh came to Jonah" is the standard introduction to prophetic books and prophetic oracles. It thus emphasizes

Jonah's role as Yahweh's prophet. What follows, however, is not Jonah's recorded preaching, but the story of his attempted flight to Tarshish. There were several cities named Tarshish. But the one that was probably Jonah's intended destination was a port on the southern shore of Spain. It was the farthest point west of Israel to which one could sail at that time. Nineveh lay to the east. In other words, Jonah tried to travel as far as he could in the opposite direction from the one Yahweh commanded him to go.

He "fled from Yahweh's presence" (v. 3). Jonah's action here seems to reflect the idea common in the ancient Middle East that each country had its own god and that each god's power was limited to his own country. But Jonah himself later confesses to the sailors that Yahweh is "the God of heaven who made the sea and the dry land" (v. 9). If he truly believes this at the beginning of the story, then his attempted flight is obviously senseless. Only in the final scene of the book does Jonah explain why he fled:

> Is this not what I said when I was still in my country? Therefore, I hurried to flee to Tarshish because I knew that you are a merciful and compassionate God, who is slow to anger, abundant in love, and repents of evil. (4:2)

Jonah did not want to preach to the Ninevites because he knew they would repent and then God would forgive them and not destroy them. But Jonah wanted Nineveh to be destroyed! His attempted flight was the ridiculous and irrational act of a desperate man. He was driven to it by the hatred he felt for the Ninevites and the fear that they would be saved from destruction. He thus acted against his better judgment and his knowledge that Yahweh's power was unlimited.

Jonah's encounter with the sailors on the ship in which he fled is remarkably ironic. In the first place, these rugged sailors, whom Jonah must have despised as foreigners, are religious men. Although they do not know Yahweh, they believe fervently in their own gods and call upon them for relief when Yahweh suddenly flings the storm at them (1:4–5a). Jonah appears less pious. He is asleep in the "bowels" of the ship (perhaps a hint of this imminent "death" in the belly of the fish). The captain awakens him and admonishes him to join the others in prayer (1:5b–6). The captain is unaware of Jonah's predicament. How can he pray to the God from whom he is trying to flee? Jonah is also less faithful. By casting lots, the sailors determine that

Jonah is the cause of the storm (1:7). In answer to their questions about him (1:8), he boasts that he is a Hebrew and that his God is Yahweh, who made sea and land (1:9). He is proud of his national, ethnic, and religious heritage. But if Jonah really believes this, how could he try to run away? The sailors, in contrast, do believe in Yahweh—immediately and at Jonah's word alone—and they are terrified (1:10). Jonah's confession in verse 9 holds a greater truth than he realizes. Yahweh is indeed the Lord of sea and dry land. But the Lord of all cares for all people and all creatures, as Jonah is about to learn.

Most ironic of all, the sailors are more righteous than Jonah. He is doing all he can to get away from preaching to the Ninevites, because he wants all of the thousands of them to perish. But the sailors do all they can, even risking their lives, to save the life of one man, Jonah (1:13). It is only when all their efforts fail, and then with cries for forgiveness for taking an "innocent" man's life, that the sailors follow Jonah's advice to "fling" him overboard (1:12–15) into the very storm that Yahweh "flings" at the ship. When the storm immediately ceases, the sailors' faith in Yahweh is deepened, and they sacrifice and make vows to him (1:16).

Act Two (1:17–2:10 [2:1–11 Heb.])

The second act takes place inside the fish. Most of it is the psalm that Jonah recites. That psalm is not entirely appropriate to Jonah's situation in the story. It does not mention the fish or any of Jonah's peculiar circumstances. It does describe being thrown into the sea, though it says that Yahweh rather than sailors cast the psalmist there (Jonah 2:3). It uses the sea in parallel with Sheol and the Pit, which are references to the underworld, the abode of the dead. All of these are metaphors for extreme suffering, perhaps disease, that brought the psalmist to the brink of death. But the psalm overall does not lament the psalmist's condition. Rather, it is a psalm of thanksgiving, praising Yahweh and expressing gratitude for having rescued the psalmist from crisis. Again, this does not fit well with the story, since Jonah, not yet rescued, recites this psalm from the belly of the fish. Thus, the psalm was evidently not composed for the story of Jonah but was borrowed from elsewhere, and may even be a later insertion into the book.

What is important for our treatment of the book is to notice that Jonah never expresses regret for his actions or his attitude. He is, perhaps, sorry that he was caught and that he was forced to spend time inside the fish, but he is not repentant. He will go to Nineveh to preach only because he has no alternative. He has learned that he cannot flee from Yahweh, but he has not changed his attitude toward the Ninevites. Obstinate and unrepentant, he remains the stereotypical bigot.

Act Three, Scene One (3:1–10)

Jonah again receives the prophetic call, as "the word of Yahweh came to him a second time," commanding him to go to Nineveh (3:1–2). This time he obeys (v. 3a), though only because he has seen the futility of trying to flee, and not because his attitude has changed. Nineveh is described as an enormous city, which would take three days to traverse (vv. 3b). The point of the city's size, as will be made clear at the end of the book (4:11) is that it is full of people.

Jonah goes a day's journey into the city and proclaims his message. It is brusque and reflects Jonah's loathing of his task: "Forty days more, and Nineveh is overthrown!" (3:4). Nevertheless, perhaps because of its curtness, the message convicts the people of Nineveh. Like the sailors earlier, these foreigners believe in God (3:5). What is more, unlike Jonah, they repent— every single one of them, from the king on down to the poorest citizen, by royal decree, in sackcloth and ashes, with fasting (3:5–9). Even the animals show more contrition than Jonah (v. 8)! All of this in the hope that maybe God will also repent and change his mind about destroying Nineveh (v. 9). And God, impressed by the people's response, does indeed halt the planned destruction (3:10).

Act Three, Scene Two (4:1–11)

Jonah is irritated and angered by all this repenting (4:1). He is annoyed and frustrated at God's merciful nature (4:2). It was God's mercy that motivated him to flee in the first place, and he has now decided that since God is so gracious, life is not worth living any longer (4:3).

Yahweh determines to try once more to teach Jonah a lesson. Just as he had designated a large fish to swallow Jonah (2:1), so now he designates a plant to grow up at the place where Jonah is watching over the city (4:6). Jonah delights in the plant and the shade that it provides him. But then God designates first a worm to kill the plant (4:7) and then a sultry wind to oppress Jonah (4:8). The repetition of the verb "designate" or "ordain" reemphasizes the point that Yahweh controls all natural forces on "the sea and the dry land." Jonah is so miserable and frustrated with the sun beating down on him that once more he wishes he were dead (4:8). He feels the same anger and discomfort at the death of the plant that he felt at Yahweh's not destroying the city of Nineveh!

Jonah defends himself at Yahweh's questioning (4:9–10). His anger, he claims, is justified. Yahweh uses Jonah's feelings of anger and frustration to try once more to get the stubborn prophet to understand divine mercy. Jonah felt sorry for the plant when it died (4:10). He is so incredibly hardhearted, so bereft of feelings for anyone but himself, that the closest Yahweh can come to communicating to him a sense of compassion is to use the plant in which Jonah has taken pleasure. The implication is that Jonah really feels sorry for himself, since he had not sown or nurtured the plant. Yahweh has a similar sense of pity and compassion for the thousands of people in Nineveh, not to mention the animals (4:11).

Conclusion

Jonah is a ludicrous, pitiful, and despicable character. His narrow prejudice and bigotry have made him that way. His story shows the ridiculous lengths to which racism can lead a person. Jonah cares for plants more than people. God's mercy angers him. Even the "heathens," who do not know the one true God, display a better sense of morality and a truer understanding of God's nature than does Jonah. The book ends with an object lesson. It records no response from Jonah to Yahweh's final question. It is not clear whether Jonah finally got the message. But the question remains open for every reader of the book. "God so loved the world" is not just an empty confession, but makes a difference in the way people of different racial, ethnic, cultural, and social backgrounds live together.

9

"Him Shall the Nations Seek"

Isaiah's Vision of Universal Harmony and Other Prophetic Texts

Until the recent "Million Man March," it was the largest rally ever to descend on Washington, D.C. Over a quarter of a million people assembled on the Washington mall in front of the Lincoln Memorial on August 28, 1963. It was the brainchild of A. Philip Randolph, in his seventies at the time, who had achieved important concessions for unemployed blacks from Roosevelt two decades earlier, by planning to conduct a large-scale protest of the same nature in the capital. Among the leaders of the march, the focus of concern in the hours immediately before the program was the speech by John Lewis, chairman of SNCC. The Archbishop of Washington considered certain statements in it to be too militant, and threatened to withdraw if they were not changed. The loss of the Catholic constituency posed a serious threat, and the speech was rewritten at the last minute, though the new version could be regarded as stronger. Today, over thirty years later, it is not Lewis's speech that is best remembered, but the famous "I have a dream" speech of Dr. Martin Luther King Jr. King's opening, "Five score years ago," was reminiscent of Lincoln's Gettysburg address. He referred to Lincoln's Emancipation Proclamation and the hope for freedom—still unfulfilled—that it had brought to African Americans. He quoted the Declaration of Independence and its yet unrealized, self-evident truth "that all men are created equal." But the document that King quoted the most, which in fact pervaded the spirit of his speech, was the Bible. Not surprisingly, King's speeches were filled with references to the Bible. He was, after all, a preacher. All the quotations and allusions in King's Washington speech are from a particular section of the Bible—the prophetic books. Again, this is not too surprising, since King was like a biblical prophet in many ways. In this chapter, we will focus on prophetic texts, specifically, two passages from Isaiah that, like King's speeches, expound a vision for the future. We will also briefly treat passages from other prophetic books, which use the Cushites as illustrations for their message.

The Nature
of Biblical Prophecy

The primary role of prophets in the Bible is not to predict the future but to preach to their contemporaries. An old adage states that they are more concerned with forthtelling than with foretelling. Most of their "predictions" are really threats about how God will punish the people of Israel and Judah in the future if they do not change their ways and live according to divine prescription. They addressed their contemporaries about social, political, and religious problems of their day, just as King did. The prophet Amos, for example, criticized the people of eighth-century Israel (ca. 750 B.C.), especially the upper classes, for their callous mistreatment of the poor. He told them that their worship of God was vain unless they would "let justice roll down like waters, and righteousness like a constant stream" (Amos 5:21–24). Twenty-seven hundred years later, King quoted Amos 5:24 in his call for fair treatment of African Americans.

At the same time, there are passages in the prophets that describe an ideal vision for the future, and King's "dream" speech shares the character and spirit of these passages as well.

"Every valley shall be exalted, every hill and mountain shall be made low; the rough places will be made plains, and the crooked places will be made straight; and the glory of the Lord shall be revealed, and all flesh shall see it together." (Isa. 40:4–5)

This text, also quoted by King, is from "Second" or "Deutero-" Isaiah. There is no book of 2 Isaiah in the Bible, but scholars use this designation for chapters 40—55 of the book of Isaiah.[7] This is because these chapters presuppose an entirely different time and set of concerns from those of the prophet Isaiah after whom the book is named. The "first" Isaiah, whose prophecies are included in chapters 1—39, was roughly a contemporary of Amos in the eighth century B.C. While Amos preached in Israel, Isaiah worked in Judah. But chapters 40—55 reflect a different setting—specifically in 539–538 B.C. The Persian king, Cyrus, has just come to power and is about to release the captives from Judah in Babylon so that they can return to Jerusalem and re-build the Temple, the city, and their lives (44:28). Thus, 40:2 says that Jerusalem's punishment is over. The quotation above, from 40:4–5, describes the preparation of the "highway in the wilderness" (v. 3) between Babylon and Jerusalem, by which the people of Judah will return. It is all part of a visionary por-trait, a "dream speech," about the glorious return of the exiles to their homeland. King used that description of the leveling of the highway to articulate his vision of equal justice in America.

Visions of
Harmony in Isaiah

Isaiah 1—39 also contains some striking visions about the future, though these are unrelated to the return from Babylon of Isaiah 40—55. One of these is a famous text shared by Isaiah and Micah (the translation below is from Isaiah, but Micah is almost identical):

> It will transpire in the latter days
>   that the mountain of Yahweh's temple
> will be established at the head of the mountains,
>   and raised above the hills.
> Then all the nations will stream to it.
>   Many peoples will come and say,
> "Come, let us go to the mountain of Yahweh,
>   to the temple of Jacob's God
> so that he may teach us his ways
>   and we can walk in his paths."
> For the law will go forth from Zion
>   and Yahweh's word from Jerusalem.
> He will judge between the nations

and decide for many peoples.
They will beat their swords into plowshares
   and their spears into pruning hooks.
Nation will not raise sword against nation,
   nor will they learn war anymore.
                    (Isa. 2:2–4‖Micah 4:1–3)

The fact that these verses envision the ideal world as one of peace between all nations led to their being inscribed on the United Nations building in New York. It is a beautiful world that is imagined, where weapons are no longer necessary and are converted to farm implements. The source of this harmony is religion. Yahweh himself adjudicates between nations, so all wars cease. Indeed, the center of it is the Temple of Yahweh in Jerusalem (also called Zion). All the nations accept Yahweh as God and flock to the Temple for religious instruction. To be sure, the vision is nationalistic and egocentric in a sense. But it is still noteworthy for our discussion of racism that the core of the ideal world and future is accord and peaceful existence among all peoples of the earth.

An even more idealized vision of peace is found just a few chapters later, in Isaiah 11:1–9.

Wolf will reside with lamb,
   leopard lie down with kid.
Calf, lion, and fatling together,
   with a small child leading them.
Cow and bear will feed;
   together their young will lie down.
   the bear will eat straw like the cow.
Nursing infant will play at viper's bore.
   Weaned child will put his hand in the serpent's hole.
They will neither harm nor destroy
   in all my holy mountain.
For the earth will be as full of the knowledge of Yahweh
   As the waters covering the sea.
                    (Isa. 11:6–9)

The peace envisioned here is more than the mere absence of conflict. It is the utter harmony entailed by the Hebrew word *shalom*. It is truly universal, as it includes all of creation. Animals that are normally enemies reside together in perfect tranquillity. The end of the world in this vision has come full circle to its beginning. This is a return to the pristine state of creation in the Garden of Eden. There is harmony of God with humans, humans with one another, humans with the animals, and the animals among themselves. What brought about the loss of this harmony on all levels, according to Genesis 2—3, was human disobedience—sin. But such harmony has remained God's intention from creation.

Again, this passage is nationalistic in its outlook. God's residence in the Garden is now the Temple in Jerusalem ("my holy mountain," v. 9). It is the royal heir of David in Jerusalem (the "shoot" or "root" of Jesse, vv. 1, 10) who brings about this situation. He is the warrior who ensures justice for the poor by slaying the wicked (vv. 3–5). Safeguarding the rights of the poor was one of the king's primary responsibilities in the ideology of monarchy in the ancient Middle East. The vision, indeed, stems from the royal theology of the Davidic dynasty in Judah. This particular text, however, was probably written in the postexilic period (after ca. 538 B.C.), since it presupposes that David's dynasty has been cut off ("stump of Jesse" in 11:1). It looks forward to a future Messianic age, "Messiah" being a royal title ("anointed") for the restored Davidic king, and describes that age in visionary terms. Christians, of course, see Jesus as the fulfillment of this Messianic expectation. Thus, Revelation 5:5 in the New Testament alludes to Isaiah 11:1–9 when it refers to Jesus as the "Root of David." But Christian theology has generally failed to stress the "horizontal" dimension of harmony among different people that is implicit in texts like Isaiah 11. Instead, Christianity has tended to focus on the "vertical" relationship of the individual to God. And Christian history, with its multiple wars and persecutions, has certainly fallen short of the ideal vision in these texts. In the following chapters of this book we will deal with New Testament texts, which evince as strong a concern for this horizontal theme as the Old Testament passages would lead us to expect. But first we must treat two specific passages from Old Testament prophets that contain references to the Cushites. These references might be considered racist and have been used that way in the past, so they require analysis in their historical and literary contexts to determine what the prophet in each case is saying to his audience.

The Cushites in
Other Prophetic Texts

"Are you Israelites not like the Cushites to me?" says Yahweh. "Did I not bring Israel up from the land of Egypt, the Philistines from Caphtor, and Aram from Qir?" (Amos 9:7)

As mentioned earlier, Amos confronted social and religious ills of the eighth-century Israelites. Because of their sins, he proclaimed that judgment from God, in the form of a devastating military defeat by a foreign power, was imminent. Amos's topic in 9:7 is election. It is a topic which surfaces earlier in the book as well. The reason is spelled out in 3:2:

> You only have I known from all the families of the earth,
> so I will visit all your guilty deeds upon you.

God's "knowing" Israel is a way of expressing relationship. Israel was Yahweh's chosen people, the only ones with whom he had a special relationship. As such, they were especially culpable for the sins they committed because they should have known better. Election carries special responsibility.

Amos 9:7 has an even stronger message about election. Israel's sins have estranged them from Yahweh to the point that he now denies any special relationship with them, denies that they are his chosen people! The verse has two parts. The first part compares the Israelites to the Cushites, the residents of Ethiopia or Nubia, who were black-skinned. But their skin color does not necessarily have anything to do with this verse.

> To compare the Israelites with the Cushites probably does not in itself mean to say anything disdainful, much less anything reprehensible, about them. They are mentioned simply as representative of foreign and remote peoples who live on the outermost periphery of the known world. If Israel is the same as they in the sight of Yahweh, then it cannot claim any kind of privileged position.[8]

The mention of Nubia (Cush) in Isaiah 18:1 as the frontier of the familiar world confirms this understanding. Amos is saying that Yahweh has come to regard the Israelites as they regard the Cushites—distant and different. As the chosen people, Israel should be closer to God than any nation, but this is not the case because their sin has alienated them from God. Israel is no more special in God's eyes than those who inhabit the remote fringe of the Middle Eastern world—the Cushites.

The second part of the verse further illustrates the point. Amos says that the exodus, in which Yahweh brought Israel up from Egypt, has nothing to do with election. It does not make Israel special, because Yahweh also directed the movements of other peoples such as the Philistines and Aramaeans. The next verse threatens the destruction of Israel. But here they are called "the sinful people" rather than "Yahweh's people." The only thing that makes them stand out is their sin, and for that reason they are now *chosen* for punishment. As part of the punishment, to add to the irony, verse 9 describes how the formerly chosen people will be scattered among the other nations.

> Can a Cushite change his skin or a leopard his spots?
>> Then you who are accustomed to doing evil could do good.
>>>>>>> (Jer. 13:23)

Unlike Amos, Jeremiah's reference to Nubians clearly has to do with skin color. Otherwise, his message in many ways is similar to Amos's. Jeremiah prophesied about two hundred years after Amos to the southern kingdom of Judah (ca. 627–580 B.C.). Just as Amos had threatened the impending destruction of Israel, which occurred under the Assyrians in 721 B.C., so Jeremiah warned that the sinfulness of Judah would bring about the destruction of Jerusalem at the hands of the Babylonians, which came about in 586 B.C. The oracle that begins in Jer. 13:20 alludes to an army invading from the north, and the verse immediately following ours (13:24) says that Yahweh will scatter Judah among the nations just as in Amos 9:9. Jeremiah's point in verse 23 is that the people of Judah have become so used to behaving wickedly that it has become part of their nature. They can no more change their sinful ways than a Nubian could change skin color or a leopard its spots. As with the Amos passage, this verse does not disparage Nubians or black-skinned people. There is nothing at all wrong or undesirable about having black skin, any more than it is undesirable for a leopard to have spots. Indeed, the examples of the Nubian and the leopard seem to have been chosen for their distinctiveness, features in which each in turn could be said to take pride. Herein lies an important difference with what Jeremiah says about the people of Judah. The characteristics of the Nubian and the leopard are innate, but the behavior of the people of Judah is learned. The word translated "accustomed" means "learned" or "taught." The people have trained themselves to do wrong, and have now become so adept at it that it is part of their nature.

part four

Christ and the Church

10

"The Spirit of the Lord Is upon Me"

The Mission of Jesus in the Gospel of Luke

Fannie Lou Hamer was a founding leader of the Mississippi Freedom Democratic Party, which sent delegates to the 1964 Democratic National Convention in Atlantic City in an effort to be seated in place of the "regular" Democratic delegates of the state. After grueling interviews by the credentials committee and intense negotiation with party leaders, they were offered the compromise solution of two at-large votes in the convention. Many considered this a victory for the M.F.D.P., but they turned it down and left the convention. "We didn't come here for no two seats when all of us is tired," replied Ms. Hamer. In her article "Sick and Tired of Being Sick and Tired," written four years later,[9] Ms. Hamer said the following:

> Now I want to say a word or two about the churches and this race situation. I travel quite a bit across the country, and a lot of the kids are asking, "Is God alive, or is he dead?" Now they *mean* it when they ask that question. They're not just trying to be smart or something like that. And I think I know what makes them ask that question: it is the hypocrites, the black and the white hypocrites, who make them ask that question. The hypocrites who do too much pretending and not enough actual working, the white ministers and the black ministers standing behind a podium and preaching a lie on Sunday. For what the kids are now asking is something like this: "If this is Christianity that is being offered in most of the churches around this

land, then we don't want any part of it. Look at what is happening all over the land, and the churches don't seem to pay any attention to it." We have almost driven our young people from God with this big act of hypocrisy. We have to take them seriously—I know I do—when they say that God is not God if he lets all these huge churches pour millions of dollars into buildings for their own people, and lets the kids in their own neighborhood go without food and without clothing and without decent shelter.

Everybody knows that the most segregated hour in America is the eleven o'clock church service. But there is something worse than that. That is when you see these white and black hypocrites in all of their fine clothes come out of a worship service, and turn up their nose at a kid in rags, or a man drunk on the street, and ask themselves, "Now what's wrong with *him?*" They never ask, "*Why* is that kid in rags?" "*Why* is that man drunk?" They never stop to think that it was something that put the kid in rags, just as it was something that drove that man to drink.

Just as it's time for America to wake up, it is long *past* time for the churches to wake up. The churches have got to say that they will have no more talk that "because your skin is a little different, you're better than they are." The churches have got to remember how Christ dealt with the poor people. He said, "The spirit of the Lord is upon me, because he hath anointed me to preach the gospel to the poor; he hath sent me to heal the brokenhearted, to preach deliverance to the captives, and recovering of sight to the blind, to set at liberty them that are bruised" (Luke 4:18). Jesus wasn't just talking about black people, or about white people, he was talking about *people*. There's no difference in people, for Paul says, "God hath made of one blood all nations of men for to dwell on all the face of the earth" (Acts 17:26). That means that whether we're white, black, red, yellow or polka dot, we're made from the same blood.

The next four chapters will trace theological themes in three different New Testament writers that relate to our topic of racism. We begin with Luke, the physician and companion of Paul (Col. 4:14; 2 Tim. 4:11; Philemon 24), who wrote both the Gospel of Luke and the book of Acts, from which Ms. Hamer quotes. Her choice of texts from Luke's works is especially appropriate, because one of the major themes in his two-volume work is that the Christian gospel is for everyone. In Acts, the first history of Christianity, Luke recounts the struggle in the early (Jewish) church over the acceptance of Gentile converts, one of whom was Luke himself. He highlights Old Testament texts, such as those treated in the last chapter, which envision the Messianic age as one of universal acceptance and harmony. In his Gospel, as Ms. Hamer suggests, Luke emphasizes Jesus' mission to Gentiles and Samaritans but also to all groups and classes of people, especially those who were outcasts in the eyes of mainline, upper-class Jewish society—women, the poor, those with physical defects and chronic illnesses, and those in certain despised professions such as tax collectors.

Luke 1:1–4   The Preface

In the preface to his Gospel, Luke tells how he went about compiling his account, reading other "narratives" of Jesus' life (1:1) and interviewing eyewitnesses (1:2). The work is written to a certain "Theophilus" (1:3), who is also the intended audience for the book of Acts (Acts 1:1). This Theophilus is otherwise unknown. The name is obviously Greek, and the fact that Luke addresses him with the title "most excellent" has led some to speculate that he was an official of some sort. This would account for Luke's generally positive portrayal of the Roman government in both Luke and Acts. Others have pointed out that the name Theophilus means "lover of God," and have proposed that it does not refer to a real person but is symbolic for any seeker of religious truth. In either case, the name indicates that Luke's audience may have been at least primarily Greek and hints at a concern on his part to show that Christianity, which began in Jewish circles, was for everyone.

Luke 1:5–2:52   Jesus' Birth

Like Matthew, Luke begins by recounting Jesus' birth. But Luke is the only Gospel that details the role of the women, Mary and Elizabeth, in the story. Jesus' birth is closely tied to that of his cousin, John the Baptist. John's mother, Elizabeth, praises God for showing special favor to her when she learns of her pregnancy in old age (1:7, 24–25). Her faith contrasts with that of her husband, Zechariah, who is incredulous at the announcement of the angel Gabriel and consequently is struck dumb until the birth (1:8–23, 62–64). It is Elizabeth who first names John (1:59–63). She is also apparently the first human to recognize who Mary's child will be (1:39–45). Gabriel also visits Mary with the announcement of her pregnancy (1:26–38). Luke alone records the visit. Mary is perplexed at the announcement, since she is not married (vv. 34–35), but she never doubts its veracity (v. 38). Luke's is also the only Gospel to include the Magnificat (1:46–55), the beautiful poem uttered by Mary when she greets Elizabeth. Finally, the story of the adolescent Jesus' visit to the Temple, which is peculiar to Luke (2:41–51), concludes by noting that Mary guarded "all these things" about Jesus in her heart.

Those who celebrate Jesus' birth in Luke's account laud his universal mission. The angels who appear to the shepherds in the vicinity of Bethlehem proclaim that his birth means "peace on earth among people of good will" (2:14). The old man, Simeon, who was awaiting a glimpse of the Messiah before his death, said that Jesus was God's salvation "prepared before all the peoples" and that he would be "a light for revelation to Gentiles [or nations]" (2:31–32).

Luke 3:23–4:30   The Beginning of Jesus' Ministry

Luke explicitly begins his account of Jesus' ministry proper in 3:23 by noting his age (about thirty) and then immediately giving his genealogy. Matthew 1:1–17 also gives a genealogy for Jesus, but the two differ in several respects. Most noteworthy is the fact that Matthew begins with Abraham and follows the line down to Jesus, while Luke begins with Jesus and traces his roots all the way back to Adam. This illustrates the different theological orientations of Matthew and Luke. Matthew, who apparently wrote for a predominantly Jewish or Jewish-Christian audience, emphasizes Jesus' Jewish origins. Not only is he a son of Abraham, but Matthew shows him to be a direct descendant of David through the royal line. Thus, Jesus is truly the Davidic Messiah or Christ (both words mean "anointed"), the "king of the Jews." Luke, however, makes another point. Jesus is descended not just from Abraham, but from Adam. He is not just

Jewish, but human, and his ministry is not just to Jews, but to all people.

Jesus was impelled to begin his ministry, according to Luke, by the Holy Spirit, who came upon him at his baptism (3:21–22). It was the Spirit who led him into the wilderness to be tempted (4:1–13), and having passed that obstacle, he returned in the power of the Spirit to his native Galilee (4:14–15). In his hometown of Nazareth on the Sabbath, he spoke on the text from Isaiah 61: "The Spirit of the Lord is upon me." He told those present in the synagogue that he had fulfilled that text. The fulfillment lay not just in the presence of the Spirit, but in the deeds he performed motivated by the Spirit: preaching good news to the poor and release to captives, restoring sight to the blind and liberty to the oppressed. He was addressing the needs of the underprivileged and disenfranchised in that society. Moreover, in his remarks on this text Jesus cited what was evidently a popular saying, "No prophet is welcome in his own country" (4:23–24). He illustrated the proverb with two Old Testament stories. Elijah and Elisha had both done miraculous deeds for non-Israelites rather than for needy people in their own country (4:25–27). He was telling his fellow citizens of Nazareth that they did not honor him because he had grown up in their midst, and so he would not do miracles there. They became furious and tried to kill him (4:28–30). This story, which Luke elaborates far more than the other Gospels, hints that most Jews would reject Jesus and points out God's loving concern for all people, Gentiles as well as Jews.

Luke 7:11–50   Jesus' Continuing Ministry

Throughout Luke's Gospel, Jesus' ministry exemplifies the interests mentioned in the episode in Nazareth. It focuses on the "undesirables" of the day. There is perhaps no better example of this than the material in chapter 7. We begin with 7:11–17, the account of Jesus' reviving the son of the widow of Nain. The episode is very similar to the stories of Elijah (1 Kings 17:17–24) and Elisha (2 Kings 4:18–37), to whom Jesus made reference in his speech in Nazareth. In fact, 1 Kings 17:11–17 is the continuation of the story about the widow of Zarephath that Jesus mentions in Luke 4:25–26. In Luke 7:18–23, John the Baptist, who has been imprisoned and is perhaps starting to doubt himself, sends some of his followers to inquire whether Jesus is indeed the promised Messiah. Jesus' answer in 7:22 echoes Isaiah 61, from which he quoted in Nazareth: the blind see, the lame walk, the lepers are cleansed, the deaf hear, the dead are raised, and the poor receive the good news. Jesus goes on to praise John's ministry (7:24–28) and thereby to justify the outcasts, like tax collectors, who had been converted by him while the religious leaders refused John and "rejected God's purpose" (7:29–30). He then contrasts John's ministry with his own (7:31–35). John was austere and demanded repentance. Jesus befriends tax collectors (like Levi, see 5:27–32, and Zacchaeus, see 19:1–10) and sinners. In the very next story (7:36–50), he allows a "sinful woman" to wash his feet and contrasts her penitence with the self-righteousness of his reluctant host.

The woman who washed Jesus' feet is just one of many women of importance in Luke. Women may have been second-class citizens in first-century Palestine, but they had a special place in Jesus' ministry according to Luke. Jesus' most loyal followers included several women, and it was they who supported him financially (8:1–3). They were the ones who discovered the empty tomb (24:1–11). The woman who was healed of her constant hemorrhage when she touched Jesus' garment (8:43–48) showed exemplary faith, greater than that of Jairus, the ruler of the synagogue whose story surrounds hers (8:40–42, 49–56). Another exemplary woman was the poor, nameless widow whose gift of two coins to the Temple treasury was all she had (21:1–4).

Luke 7:1–10   The Centurion's Slave

In this context of Jesus' mission to the lower rungs of the social ladder, two stories dealing with non-Jews stand out. In the first, an unnamed Roman centurion had a beloved slave who became quite ill, so he sent to ask for Jesus' help. Jesus headed toward his house, but the centurion would not permit him to enter. He showed a good understanding of Jesus' power and authority. "Just say the word and my servant will be healed" (or "let my servant be healed") was the message he sent to Jesus. Jesus was amazed. "Not even in Israel have I found such faith!" he said. The prime example of faith in Luke comes not from an Israelite but from a Gentile, a Roman soldier.

Luke 17:11–19   The Samaritan Leper

In Jesus' day, Jews despised Samaritans. The prejudice was ethnic as well as religious. Jews regarded Samaritans as foreigners whose religion was a perversion of legitimate Judaism. The animosity was so great that most Jews would have nothing to do with Samaritans, even going to the extreme of walking miles out of their way in order to avoid passing through Samaritan territory. Samaritans reciprocated by refusing to serve food or drink to anyone on the way toward Jerusalem.

Luke 17:11–19 tells of Jesus' encountering ten lepers in a village on the outskirts of Samaria. Leprosy was a horrible, disfiguring disease. Being afflicted with it then was like having cancer or AIDS today. Since it was considered incurable and highly contagious, its victims were quarantined and socially ostracized. They were called "unclean," and were required to shout this word whenever they approached other people. The ten lepers whom Jesus met had heard of him. As they kept their distance they asked for his help: "Have mercy on us!" (17:12–13). Jesus told them to show themselves to the priests. Priests were in charge of declaring persons to be "clean," that is, cured of leprosy. As they went in search of a priest, their disease disappeared and they were healed (17:14). Only one of the ten, however, returned to thank Jesus and to praise God for his newfound health. He was a Samaritan (17:16). Jesus expressed dismay that "this foreigner" alone had returned to praise God (17:17–18). There was nothing wrong with being a Samaritan, but Jesus hoped for more from his own people. As with the Roman centurion's example of faith, the prime example of gratitude in Luke also comes from a non-Jew. But the Samaritan's gratitude was also a show of faith. He made the connection between Jesus' deed and his identity. He recognized the hand of God, whom he praised.

Luke 10:25–37   The Good Samaritan

As in his healing ministry, so in Jesus' teachings in Luke the "undesirable" elements of society, such as the poor, have a special place. Thus, Luke's version of the beatitude reads "Blessed are you poor, for yours is the kingdom of God" (6:20), whereas Matthew has "Blessed are the poor in spirit . . ." (Matt. 5:3); and

Luke's Jesus pronounces a corresponding "Woe to you who are rich . . ." (6:24), which is lacking in Matthew. In Luke 14:12–14, Jesus counsels his host to invite the poor and physically deformed—those who cannot repay him—to his banquets, so as to build credit with God.

In one of his teachings, the famous parable of the "good Samaritan," Jesus counters exactly the kind of prejudice that racism represents. The parable is unique to Luke, and furthers his theme of God's love in Christ being for all people. But it is more than a story with the bland moral of "Be nice to everyone." It has a sharp edge, which Jesus wielded with skill against his opponents. The parable subtly and brilliantly undermines attitudes of prejudice by forcing his inquisitors to commend their enemies and thus denounce their own bias. Since the hero in the parable is a Samaritan, its message is again about both ethnic and religious prejudice.

The context of the parable is set in 10:25–28. A "lawyer" asks Jesus a question. The profession of this lawyer is not quite the same as that we know today. He is rather someone versed in the Old Testament law, and is seen therefore as an authority as much in religious matters as in secular ones. His motive in raising the question is not sincere. He does not seek to learn from Jesus but to test him, presumably in order to find some grounds to criticize him. He asks, "What should I do to inherit eternal life?" Jesus turns the question back on the man: "What is written in the law? How do you read?" This is to say, "You are the expert in the law. You tell me." The lawyer has the chance to demonstrate his expertise and must give a straight answer. His response is a recitation of Deuteronomy 6:5: "You shall love the Lord your God with all your heart, soul, strength, and mind."[10] This verse follows what is known as the *shema'*, "Hear, O Israel, Yahweh is our God, Yahweh alone." These two verses make up the confession that constitutes Israel's national and religious identity. The lawyer's answer, in other words, is an expression of ethnic and religious pride. He adds, "And [you shall love] your neighbor as yourself," which is not an integral part of the confession in Deuteronomy, but derives from Leviticus 19:18.

The combination of these two quotations makes it apparent that the lawyer seeks to use them to limit the people of God by excluding those whom he regards as ethnically and religiously unacceptable. In the context of the confession of Israel's national identity, the "neighbor" can only be his fellow Jews. Those of other ethnic origins are excluded; but not all Jews are acceptable, either. Deuteronomy 6:4–5 stands at the beginning of the law of Moses in Deuteronomy and introduces an injunction to keep all of the law and teach it to future generations (6:6–9). In fact, keeping the law fervently would seem to be what it means to love God, at least in Deuteronomy. Hence, those who do not keep the law are excluded on religious grounds. Since the lawyer is in charge of studying the law, he and others like him draw the lines determining what is proper interpretation and practice of the law and what is not. He and his colleagues decide whom to accept and whom to reject on religious grounds.

Despite the lawyer's narrow interpretation, the answer he has given is a good one. One should love God and one's neighbor. So Jesus approves of his answer (10:28). But the lawyer now appears rather foolish for having answered his own question and has exposed his insincerity by showing that he had an answer all along. So he continues the dialogue in an effort to "justify himself," or to save face. Perhaps he also wanted vindication for his interpretation of the law or to have Jesus admit that he (the lawyer) was one of the righteous. He asks another question: "Just who is my neighbor?" He must have been thinking that he had Jesus where he wanted him. If Jesus indicated that only Jews fit in the category of neighbor, he would be in agreement with the lawyer's narrow interpretation and exclude those among whom he had gained a following. If, on the other hand, Jesus were to give an explicitly inclusive definition of neighbor—that it means all people—he would seem to be downplaying the importance of keeping the law's commandments, which would be tantamount to a denial of Judaism. It seemed that Jesus was trapped.

As on other occasions when Jesus is facing a seemingly unanswerable question, he replies with a parable. Like all parables, the story that comprises it is drawn from everyday life and could have actually occurred. In this instance, Jesus tells of a man going from Jerusalem to Jericho, who is robbed, beaten, and left to die. The story is quite possible and presumes a common occurrence. The road between Jerusalem and Jericho passed through rugged and barren country, which held many hideouts for bandits and ruffians. It was notorious for the danger it posed to travelers.

It is in the details about those who encounter the injured man that the parable becomes pointed. First a priest passing by (v. 31) and then a Levite (v. 32) come upon the man, but both continue on their journeys without stopping to help. Jesus does not explain why they do not stop. Perhaps they are afraid for their own safety. Perhaps they are in a hurry. Perhaps they think that the man is already dead and are concerned that touching him will make them ritually unclean. What is important is not their reasons for continuing on, but their identity. They are religious leaders. They are like the lawyer. They have the right ethnic pedigree and the right religious beliefs. If anyone would make his list of those who are acceptable to God, priests and Levites would. But as Jesus forces the lawyer to admit momentarily, in his parable the priest and Levite are not neighbors.

Then a Samaritan comes along. If the lawyer could have excluded anyone from his list, he would have excluded Samaritans. He probably hated them worse than Gentiles. At least the Gentiles did not claim to be part of the chosen people. Samaritans worshiped Yahweh and thought of themselves as part of Israel. But in the eyes of the lawyer and those like him the Samaritans were heathens and apostates. The Samaritan in Jesus' parable is remarkable. Without regard to the injured man's ethnicity, he has compassion for him and helps him (v. 33). He tends to the man's wounds the best that he can and then carries him to an inn for better nursing (v. 34). He pays for the man's lodging and medical expenses—two denarii, about two days' wages—and promises to reimburse the innkeeper for any other expenses he incurs (v. 35).

Then Jesus turns the conversation back to the lawyer. He does not respond directly to the lawyer's question but again forces him to answer himself: "Which of these three in your opinion proved neighbor to the man who fell among the thieves?" Jesus has changed the lawyer's question. The lawyer initially asked, "Who is my neighbor?" He was interested in drawing lines between those he must treat as peers and neighbors and those he could scorn as enemies and inferiors. But in Jesus' parable the potential neighbors are not those who are befriended, but those who are in a position to befriend; they are the doers rather than the recipients of neighborly deeds. The lawyer is made to identify with the man in need. The lawyer knows he has been manipulated by Jesus, and his response to Jesus' question barely masks his resentment. He cannot bring himself to say "the Samaritan" but instead replies, "The one who treated him with mercy" (v. 37). Then comes the final insult. Jesus tells the lawyer, "Go and do likewise." In answer to his request to identify his neighbor Jesus has held up a Samaritan and said, "Be like him." There is, of course, a moral lesson here that one should treat all people as neighbors regardless of ethnicity (or race), religion, or social status. But the lesson has a razor-sharp edge on its other side: prejudice of any kind is foolish and wrong; the person who is ruled by it is unacceptable to God.

Luke 24:36–53   To All Nations

Luke closes his Gospel by recounting Jesus' postresurrection appearances and his ascension. He then begins his second volume, Acts, by overlapping the accounts of Jesus' reunion with his disciples in Jerusalem and his ascension. After two of the disciples encounter Jesus on a journey from Jerusalem to the nearby village of Emmaus, they return to Jerusalem, where they find the eleven apostles gathered and inform them that they have seen Jesus (24:13–35). Jesus suddenly appears in the midst of the gathering and proves to them that he is alive "in the flesh" (24:36–43). He begins to instruct them about Old Testament scripture, showing them that his death and resurrection have "fulfilled" it (24:44–46). The next step is that the salvation he has thus procured, forgiveness of sins, "should be preached in his [the Messiah's] name to all the nations [or Gentiles] beginning from Jerusalem" (24:47). Another possible reading is "Beginning from Jerusalem, you are witnesses of these things" (24:48). In either case, the good news of Jesus is to go forth from Jerusalem to the entire world. The capstone to the Gospel of Luke is that fellowship with God is no longer limited to one people; salvation in Christ is available for everyone.

11

"Nothing Common or Unclean"

Growing Pains of the Early Church in the Book of Acts

He was short, thin, quick as a rabbit, and wore thick glasses. His name was James. He was black, and he was my friend. He stopped being my friend one day in eighth-grade science class. It was the spring of 1968. Momentous events were taking place in Memphis, but that was a world away at the time—for me. I had seen news footage on TV of black people being chased by dogs and sprayed by water cannon, but that was the South. In the West, where we lived, those things weren't a problem—for us at any rate.

Maybe it was from TV that I learned the word. I knew it was an insult, but it didn't mean anything—to me. In science class on that spring day in 1968 James and I had gotten into an argument. I don't remember what it was about. All I know is that I suddenly became very angry, and that's when I said it, the word that ruined my friendship with James. I can still see the look on his face the moment it came out of my mouth. It hung in the space between us, with his eyes fixed upon it in shock, hurt, and rage. "White trash!" he responded automatically. But that name meant nothing to me. It did not cut me to the quick as my insult had him. He turned away. We spoke no more that day or for several days thereafter. In truth, I don't recall ever speaking to James after that, though I am sure I must have, even if it was no longer as a friend. My family moved away a few months later, and I never saw James again. I heard later that in high school and college James became a member of a militant organization that advocated separatism from white society and violence against it. I have never doubted that my betrayal contributed to his choice. It was the one and only time I ever called anyone "nigger."

The early church, as described in the book of Acts, Luke's second volume, also struggled with ethnic differences. Specifically, the first Christians, who were Jews, were uncertain about preaching the gospel to the Gentiles. Even though they believed Jesus to be the Messiah in fulfillment of Old Testament passages like Isaiah 2:2–4 and Micah 4:1–3 and Isaiah 11:1–9, they did not immediately perceive the significance of the universal harmony in those visions for their new movement. In Acts, Luke shows how God's own intervention in the controversy left no doubt about the acceptance of Gentiles. Luke, himself a Gentile writing at a later date, wishes to make clear that from the beginning the will of God was that the gospel be available to people of all races.

Jerusalem and Judea

Acts 1:8   "You Will Be My Witnesses"

Luke begins his account of the church where he ended his story of Jesus—with his postresurrection appearance to the disciples and his ascension. Acts 1:1–9 overlaps with Luke 24:44–53. The disciples, not fully grasping Jesus' mission and thus still expecting him to establish an earthly kingdom, ask, "Will you now restore the kingdom to Israel?" Jesus replies that God's timetable is not their business (Acts 1:7), but that they are called to be witnesses to Jesus in Jerusalem, Judea, Samaria, and to the end of the earth (1:8). This reply serves as a sort of outline for the book of Acts as he traces the spread of Christianity in ever-widening, concentric circles through Palestine and Syria, to Asia Minor, and finally to Rome itself

Acts 2:1–47   Each in His Own Native Tongue:
The Beginning of the Church

The second chapter of Acts records the famous "day of Pentecost" sermon of Peter, when in a sense the church began. The beginning was signaled by the falling of the Spirit on the disciples just as the Spirit had come on Jesus at the beginning of his ministry (Luke 3:21–22; 4:1, 14). Because Pentecost was an important Jewish holiday, there were pious Jews "from every nation under heaven" staying in Jerusalem (Acts 2:5). While they shared an ethnic and religious heritage, their national origins and citizenships were diverse. So were their native languages. Hence, it was remarkable that each person heard the disciples speaking in his (these were all or almost all men) own native language (2:6–11). As a number of scholars have observed, theologically this story is a reversal of the Tower of Babel episode of Genesis 11. There, God separated the languages because of human sin. But in Acts a new act of God brings people together. In Christ the barriers of language and culture are overcome. The intensity of the fellowship of the new Christians, described at the end of the chapter, illustrates the strength of their new unity.

Twice in the course of the sermon he preaches on Pentecost, Peter refers to the universal invitation of the gospel. His quotation from the prophet Joel contains the line, "Whoever calls on the name of the Lord shall be saved" (Acts 2:21; cf. Joel 2:32). Then, toward the end of the sermon, he says that the promise [of salvation] is "to all who are far off, whomever the Lord our God calls" (2:39). Peter did not comprehend the full significance of his own words and the true breadth of the promise's validity. In the context of this speech to the "men of Israel" on Pentecost, he must still have been thinking only of Jews, albeit Jews in all parts of the world. However, it would soon be made clear to him that God's intention for the gospel was much larger.

Acts 6:1   Cultural Differences: Hellenists and Hebrews

Anytime people of different backgrounds come together for any cause or purpose, frictions are bound to emerge. The early church was no exception. The first such friction was a hint of others that would arise in the future. The initial followers of Jesus had been more or less homogeneous in cultural and ethnic background, but as the church grew it became more diverse. That growing diversity is reflected in Acts 6:1, where those of Hellenistic background began to complain that they were being treated unfairly. These Hellenists were Jews who had adopted Greek culture and were Greek speaking, as opposed to those Jews who spoke Aramaic and had resisted absorption into broader Greek culture. There were converts to Christianity from both groups.

The specific complaint of the Hellenists was that the contributions to aid widows were not being distributed equitably, so that those of Hellenistic background were being neglected. The complaint was legitimate, and when it came to the apostles they determined it was necessary to act. Several points about the course of action they adopted are telling for our study. First, the apostles wanted to find a fair solution to the problem. They therefore asked the disciples to choose seven men to take charge of the matter (6:3). To judge from their names, which are all Greek, the seven who were chosen were apparently Hellenists (6:5). A second point, then, is that the apostles, most of whom were Hebrews rather than Hellenists, did not demand uniformity in culture or political orientation. Third, they themselves were occupied with preaching the word of God and did not want to surrender that responsibility to "serve tables" (6:2). For them, faith in Christ was the most important thing, and the umbrella of Christianity was wide enough to encompass different cultures and viewpoints peacefully.

Samaria

Acts 8:1b–25   The Preaching of Philip

Two of the seven special servants chosen in chapter 6 are renowned in Acts for their preaching, and their ministries are related. Stephen's sermon, reiterated in chapter 7, so angered his audience that he became the church's first martyr. His death initiated the persecution of the church led by Saul (8:1b–3). But in the overall scheme of the book of Acts, it had an important benefit. The disciples had been caught up in the excitement of their new life and new movement and had neglected Jesus' words about being his witnesses to the world beyond. Now, though, they were scattered throughout Judea and Samaria (8:1), and as they scattered they spread the word of Christ.

Philip's success in Samaria is documented (8:4–6). What is particularly important is the confirmation of his message through signs (8:6) showing decisively that God accepts Samaritans as well as Jews. Furthermore, when Peter and John visit the Samaritan Christians to lay hands on them, the Holy Spirit falls on them just as it fell on the Jewish disciples in Jerusalem at the beginning. The message is clear: there is no difference in God's eyes between Jews and Samaritans. Both are full members of the new salvation community. Luke summarizes the church's growth to this stage in 9:31: "The church throughout all Judea, Galilee, and Samaria had peace. It increased, being built up and continuing in the fear of the Lord and the comfort of the Holy Spirit."

To All the World

Acts 8:26–40   The First Gentile Convert

The first Gentile convert to Christianity according to Acts was a black man. There had been cases of proselytes (i.e., ethnic Gentiles converted to Judaism) who became Christians, such as Nicolaus (Acts 6:5). But the first Gentile to become a Christian without first becoming a Jew was the Ethiopian official in Acts 8. The brief description of this man in 8:27–28 indicates that he was an extraordinary individual. He was an Ethiopian or Nubian and therefore a black man. He was a government official, minister of treasure for the queen of Ethiopia ("Candace" was not a name but a royal title). He was, therefore, trusted and trustworthy. He was wealthy, traveling in his own chariot with a private driver. He was cultured and well educated. Philip, who had been sent directly to the man by divine order (8:26), found him reading (in Greek? or Hebrew?) from his own copy of the book of Isaiah. He was also a very pious man, having traveled all the way from Ethiopia to Jerusalem to worship. What makes this even more extraordinary is that the man was a eunuch. According to Deuteronomy 23:1, this condition would have prevented him from participating fully in the Temple worship for which he had traveled such a great distance. This explains his hopeful question in 8:36: "What hinders my being baptized?" For a man whose physical condition as a eunuch and Gentile—both matters beyond his control—had kept him from full communion with God and his fellow believers all his life, the good news preached by Philip must have seemed almost too good to be true. He had listened intently to

Philip's message and believed it instantly. So, when he learned that faith was the only criterion for salvation[11] regardless of his physical nature, he had his chariot stopped and was baptized on the spot.

Luke says nothing more about the new convert other than "he went on his way rejoicing" (8:39). He was the beginning of the thriving Christian church in Ethiopia. Luke's account in the book of Acts turns west and follows the church's growth toward Rome, the heart of the empire. If the early evangelists had chosen a different strategy, the center of Christianity might well have been in Africa rather than in Rome.[12] Nevertheless, the Ethiopian's conversion contains a very important lesson about the all-inclusive nature of the Christian religion. Persons of every race are eligible to be full members. Physical features such as skin color, wholeness of body, or health have no bearing on one's acceptability before God. The door to the kingdom was (and is) wide open. The challenge was (and is) to get this point across to the community of the saints. The issue would come to a head with the next conversion of a Gentile reported by Luke (Acts 10). Luke places more stress on the second Gentile conversion because it had a greater impact on the early church and because the convert, Cornelius, was a Roman centurion. But the place of priority as the first Gentile convert still belongs to the African official.

Acts 9:15 My Instrument before the Gentiles: The Conversion of Saul of Tarsus

Before recounting the next Gentile conversion, Luke sets the stage for it by telling about the man who more than anyone else would evangelize the Gentile world. Saul was introduced at the end of chapter 7 as the ringleader of those who stoned Stephen (7:58). He took charge of the early persecution in Jerusalem (8:3), and as the church spread to Judea, Samaria, and beyond, Saul followed threateningly (9:1).

Saul's conversion came as he was on his way to Damascus to arrest Christians there and return them to Jerusalem for trial (9:1–2). Christ appeared to him and told him to await further instructions (9:3–6). The bright light that was part of Christ's appearance blinded Saul so that he waited for three days in the dark in Damascus (9:7–9). When a Christian in Damascus named Ananias was told by the Lord in a vision to go to Saul so that he could recover his sight, Ananias objected that he had heard of Saul's devastating persecution (9:10–14). But he was told to go anyway because Saul was God's "chosen instrument" to bring the name of the Lord "before Gentiles and kings and the children of Israel" (9:15). The mission to the Gentiles was about to begin in earnest.

Acts 10:1–11:18   Nothing Common or Unclean: The Conversion of Cornelius and Its Repercussions

Since the conversion of the Ethiopian eunuch was an isolated incident in the ministry of Philip, who was fleeing Jerusalem, it escaped the notice of the early Christian leaders in that city. But the conversion of Cornelius and the Greeks in Antioch raised the issue of the status of Gentile Christians, particularly in regard to the practice of circumcision.

Cornelius was a Roman soldier, a centurion by rank, who was stationed in Palestine in the city of Caesarea. He was also one of those known as "God-fearers" (10:1–2), that is, Gentiles who devoutly worshiped the God of Israel but who had never officially become proselytes to Judaism by undergoing the procedure of circumcision. An angel, who appeared to Cornelius during one of his prayer times, told him to send for Peter, who was staying in Joppa (10:3–8).

Meanwhile, Peter was having a vision of his own (10:9–16). He saw a large sheet-like object lowered from heaven. It contained all kinds of unclean animals, that is, animals that could not be sacrificed or eaten according to Old Testament law. Peter was told to "arise, kill and eat," but he declined, saying, "By no means, Lord, for I have never eaten anything common or unclean." The vision came to him three times, as a way of reinforcing its importance, but its meaning was not explained. He was puzzling over its significance when the envoys from Cornelius arrived, and the Holy Spirit told him to accompany them (10:20). The vision and the Spirit's command were important, because Peter was breaking Jewish taboos by having anything to do with the messengers. He had hosted them and was now on his way to meet and stay with their master. He had begun to understand the point of his vision—that other people were not "common" or "unclean" in God's view and that he should not think of them that way (10:28–29).

After hearing Cornelius relate the vision that had led him to send for Peter (10:30–33), the apostle began to preach the story of Jesus. He prefaced his remarks by saying that he now understood that "God is not one to show partiality, but in every nation whoever fears him and does right is acceptable" (10:34–35). Before Peter could finish, however, the Holy Spirit came upon the listeners (10:44). The Jews who were present were amazed because they understood what the Spirit's presence meant. This was the Gentile Pentecost. The Spirit came upon them just as the Spirit had come upon Jesus at the beginning of his ministry and upon the Jewish disciples on the day of Pentecost. They spoke in tongues just as the Jews had at the beginning of the church (10:45). This could only mean that Gentiles were suitable candidates for salvation just as much as Jews. The coming of the Spirit left no doubt about God's acceptance. Peter asked, "Can anyone forbid water for baptizing these people who have received the Holy Spirit just as we have?" (Acts 10:47). The question was rhetorical. No one could forbid baptism for the Gentiles because God had already approved them.

Baptizing Gentiles was still new, so it was inevitable that Peter's actions would come under fire. When news of Cornelius's household reached the leaders in Jerusalem, Peter was called in to justify what had happened, especially by those called the "circumcision party," that is, the group that advocated maintaining segregation between Jews and Gentiles (11:1–3). They asked, accusingly, why Peter had fellowshipped and even eaten with uncircumcised Gentiles. Peter's defense was simple. He had done what God told him to do. He recounted his vision, with its message that there was no longer any "common or unclean" person (11:4–10). He also told of his journey with Cornelius's servants to his house at the direction of God (11:11–14). Peter's most forceful argument, though, was the gift of the Holy Spirit to the Gentiles, just as to the Jews. "God gave the same gift to them as to us when we believed in the Lord Jesus Christ" (11:17). So the conversion of Gentiles was not really Peter's doing. It was God's. Peter had no choice in the matter. "Who was I that I could withstand God?" To deny the gospel to any group of people or to segregate any group as inferior or second-class citizens of the kingdom is to withstand God! The Jews present at Peter's explanation recognized that it was God and not Peter who had made the decision to admit Gentiles, and they rejoiced in it (11:18).

Acts 11:19–26
Cornelius Not Alone: The Greeks in Antioch

When the first Christians scattered from Jerusalem in the wake of Stephen's martyrdom, they spread the word about Jesus as they went. These were Jewish Christians, and they spoke to Jews in synagogues and elsewhere. But about the same time as Cornelius's conversion, some Jewish Christians, who were probably Hellenists, in Antioch began to tell the Greeks there about Jesus, and the Greeks believed in large numbers (11:19–21). When the Jerusalem leadership learned of this, they sent Barnabas to investigate. As with Peter and Cornelius's household, Barnabas saw that "the hand of the Lord was with them" (Acts 11:21) so that he was convinced that the "grace of God" (v. 23) had genuinely been given to the Gentiles as well as to Jews.

Acts 13:13–52:   To the Jew First
and Also to the Greek: Paul's Modus Operandi

Luke's account of the beginning of the church in Antioch of Pisidia in chapter 13 illustrates Saul's (now called Paul) approach to mission activity wherever he went. He entered the synagogue on the Sabbath (13:14), and then took advantage of the open invitation to speak (13:15–16) in order to preach about Jesus. His began with a recitation of Israel's historical traditions (13:17–22). With the mention of David, Paul introduced Jesus and recounted his life story as the fulfillment of Old Testament scripture and the Messianic expectation (13:23–41). Many of the Jews and proselytes were persuaded by the message and followed Paul and his comrades (13:42–43). But some viewed it as a threat and mounted an opposition (13:45). In response, Paul announced that he was turning to the Gentiles, citing Isaiah 49:6: "I have set you as a light to the Gentiles [or "nations"] to be salvation to the end of the earth" (13:47), and the Gentiles in turn rejoiced to be included (13:48). This pattern rehearses Luke's structural scheme for the entire book of Acts and one of its primary messages. The gospel of Jesus Christ is for all people. It spread first among the Jews, in Jesus' Palestinian homeland, and from there to persons of every race and ethnicity in the world.

Acts 15:1–35: The Watershed: The Jerusalem Conference

Despite the success of the gospel among the Gentiles and even the signs from God that accompanied their early conversions, full acceptance of them was difficult for some Jewish Christians. These people, who came to be known as "Judaizers," insisted that the Gentiles had to go through Moses to get to Christ, that is, they had to follow the Mosaic law, particularly the custom of circumcision, in order to attain full salvation (15:1). These teachers came, not surprisingly, from Judea, but they followed the church as it grew and spread their doctrine among the Gentile converts. When they reached Antioch, they stirred up quite a controversy, so great that the church there decided to send Paul and Barnabas to Jerusalem for a decisive answer about the matter.

In the meeting of the apostles and elders in Jerusalem there were two principal speakers whose words Luke records—Peter and James. Peter recalled his experience in preaching to Cornelius's household. God's will in the matter was clear, he said, from the fact that the Holy Spirit had come on the Gentiles just as it had on the Jewish disciples at Pentecost (15:8). Thus, God "made no distinction between us and them" (15:9). Both groups, Jew and Gentile alike, would be saved by the grace of the Lord Jesus (15:11).

After Paul and Barnabas had confirmed Peter's words by recounting God's continuing "signs and wonders" among the Gentiles, especially in Antioch (15:12), James offered a compromise solution. He began by citing a version of Amos 9:11–12.[13] The quotation refers to the reestablishment of the Davidic dynasty by the Messiah (rebuilding the dwelling or booth of David) in order that all the Gentiles (or nations) may seek the Lord. The implication of this quotation and James's use of it is staggering: the purpose for sending Christ was that the Gentiles might seek the one true God. Since God's plan all along was to bring Gentiles into fellowship with Jews as adherents of God, the Gentiles must be accepted as full members in Christ's kingdom. James goes on to suggest, therefore, that in order to further this fellowship the Gentiles be encouraged to refrain from practices that were common in Greek and Roman culture but were especially offensive to Jews (v. 20; cf. v. 29). These prohibitions seem to be drawn largely from Leviticus 17—18 and are mainly dietary regulations. They included eating meat that was "sacrificed" or dedicated to other gods (called "pollutions of idols" in v. 20) and the eating of blood (which included meat that was slaughtered by strangling since the blood was not drained from the carcass). The prohibition against eating blood derived from the covenant with Noah (Gen. 9:4), not from the law of Moses, and was thus regarded by Jews as universal in application. The remaining injunction against "unchastity" probably refers to sexual relations with family members that were common among Gentiles but considered incestuous by Jews. The Jerusalem leaders adopted James's proposal and sent a letter to the Gentile churches by the hand of Barnabas and Silas.

This conference and the decision it reached is a watershed in the book of Acts. Acts 1—15 clearly shows that in Jesus Christ, God has called all people into fellowship with him, so the Jerusalem leadership could reach only one conclusion about the acceptance of Gentiles into the church. Since God had already accepted them fully by giving them the Holy Spirit, Jewish Christians could do no less than welcome them as equals into the community of faith. The instructions that were sent out from Jerusalem were intended to facilitate fellowship between Jewish and Gentile Christians by encouraging the Gentiles to avoid practices that would be particularly offensive to Jews. The remarkable thing about the conference, especially James's speech, is the very important place that it assigns to human fellowship as God's goal in sending Christ to earth. Despite this, Christians in the subsequent centuries have not generally attached the same degree of importance to this horizontal aspect of Christian community, but have been content with severed communities and limited or hindered communion. The emphasis has been on the individual's relationship with God rather than on one's relationship with others. But perhaps the first is impossible without the second (Matt. 5:23–24).

The controversy resolved in Acts 15 is important for another reason. The question before the conference was not just the theoretical acceptance of non-Jews into the church. It was whether Gentiles were to be accepted *as they were*—uncircumcised—into the church on a level *equal* with Jewish Christians. It was therefore an issue of diversity as much as unity. The Jewish Christians who wanted the Gentiles to be circumcised were uncomfortable with the diversity they offered. These Judaizers wanted the Gentiles to become like them. It is against this background that Luke presented the message of Acts. The conference could reach only one conclusion. The events leading up to it left no room for doubt. God gave the Holy Spirit to the Gentiles (Acts 10:44–47; 11:15–18). Barnabas witnessed the "hand of the Lord" among the Gentiles. Peter, Paul, and Barnabas testified to the conference about what God had already done among the Gentiles. It was clear, therefore, that God had already accepted the Gentiles *as they were*. God welcomed not only all people, but the diversity they brought as well.

Paul left the Jerusalem conference to return to his ministry among the Gentiles. In Acts 17:22–31, the sermon quoted by Fannie Lou Hamer at the beginning of the preceding chapter, Paul preaches to a Greek audience in Athens who do not share the background of his usual Jewish audiences. As in our chapter on creation, he observes that all people share a common ancestor and are therefore related as brothers and sisters (v. 26). He also notes, in line with what we have learned about wisdom, that the creation provides "natural" revelation for all people (vv. 27–28) and testifies to God, whom the Athenians worship as unknown, as the Lord of heaven and earth and the fundamental principle for all living things (17:24–25). But the decision of the Jerusalem conference did not halt the efforts of the Judaizers; and Paul would spend a great deal of his ministry combating them on essentially the same issue faced by that conference, as we shall see in a future chapter.

part five

The Mandate
to Integrate

12

"That They May All Be One"

Unity and Fellowship
in the Writings of John

Three years of my boyhood were spent in a small New Mexico town while my father gently shepherded an aging and diminishing congregation through the process of a merger with another church in town. There was also a "colored" congregation in the community, which by coincidence had hired a new minister also named McKenzie, who arrived in town about the same time my family did. He and his wife quickly became our favorite houseguests. If we visited their home less often, it was only because they were newlyweds while my parents had four energetic boys. There were running jokes about how we were brothers and sisters but not kin, related but not by blood, and it was not unusual for us to receive each other's telephone calls. Visits to each other's churches, however, were rare and limited to special occasions, and the possibility of a merger between our two congregations was never broached. They were on opposite sides of town. When I first saw the facilities of the "colored church"—the small building and the folding chairs instead of pews—I asked why they did not just join us and was told, "They want it this way." In fact, everyone was clearly more comfortable with things as they were.

In this chapter and the next, I propose to revisit the question of my youth by putting forward, perhaps still naively, the provocative thesis that the New Testament makes a strong theological case against segregation of churches along racial lines. To put it in the strongest terms, from the perspective of New Testament authors like John and Paul, segregation is not just undesirable, but is an affront to God and defeats the very purpose for which Christ came to earth.

The Gospel of John

The Prologue (John 1:1–18)

Like Luke, the Gospel of John traces Jesus' roots back to creation, though in a very different way. John does not give a genealogy for Jesus, as do Matthew and Luke. Instead, the Gospel of John begins with a prologue on Jesus' spiritual origins. Its language is reminiscent of the creation account in Genesis 1: "In the beginning was the Word, and the Word was with God, and the Word was God." John refers to Jesus as the "Word" (Greek *logos*). The allusion to Genesis 1:1 is obvious. Throughout the creation account in Genesis 1, God creates by means of the spoken word: "God said, 'Let there be . . .'; and there was . . . " Hence, "All things came into being through him" (John 1:3) and "in him was life" (1:4). John is also probably playing on the idea of the word of God that inspires the biblical writers and characters. But in addition to these "Hebrew" notions of the word, John is alluding to the idea, common in Greek philosophy, of the *logos* as the fundamental and all-pervasive principle of the universe. Thus, nothing has come into being without the Word (1:3). The point is that John styles his message in such a way that it will be comprehensible and appealing to both Jews and Greeks.

John's message about the Word stresses its universal applicability. He states specifically that the life brought by the Word was the light of all people (1:4). The world was created through the Word, so the world belonged to the Word. The Word came to the world as one of its own (1:10). The Word's own people did not accept him (1:11)—an allusion to Jesus' rejection by his own, similar to the passage in Luke 4:16–30, which we treated in chapter 10. But to everyone who did receive him, the Word gave the potential to be reborn as a child of God (John 1:12–13). John says nothing about restrictions based on ethnicity or anything else. The way into the kingdom is open to all. John goes on to say that the Word became flesh. He does not specify any particular "brand" or race of flesh. In v. 17 he contrasts the law given through Moses with the grace and truth given through Jesus Christ. Thus, the "we" in v. 16, who have all received "grace upon grace," refers not just to Jews but to all people. Just as "all flesh" in the world were created through the Word, so the hope offered through the Word is available to all persons, of any ethnic identity.

The Woman at the Well (4:1–42)

Unlike Luke, which tells of several encounters between Jesus and non-Jews, in the Gospel of John, Jesus deals almost exclusively with his compatriots. One striking exception is the story in John 4 of the Samaritan woman whom Jesus meets at the town well. Ethnic and religious prejudice provide important background to this story. We have already described the strong animosity that existed between Jews and Samaritans in Jesus' day. The hatred was so strong that Jews traveling north from Jerusalem to Galilee generally preferred to bypass Samaria altogether. This meant lengthening their journey considerably, because they would have to travel to the Jordan River, cross it, travel north on the eastern side of the river, and then cross it again to enter Galilee (see a map of ancient Palestine). The Samaritans reciprocated this hatred. Typically, Samaritan businesses (vendors, inns, etc.) would serve travelers headed away from Jerusalem but refuse service to anyone going toward that city. Of course, Jews and Samaritans tried to avoid dealing with each other at all and certainly did not socialize.

On this particular occasion, Jesus and his disciples did pass through Samaria and stopped at the town of Sychar (4:5). He sat to rest near the town well while his disciples went in search of food (4:6, 8). Drawing water in that society was customarily "women's work," so there was nothing strange about a woman coming to the well while Jesus was there (4:7). The time of day when she came, however, about noon according to v. 6, seems somewhat unusual. Drawing water was hard work, and one would expect that women would usually come early in the morning when it was cooler. Some have suggested that this woman came later in the day because she was ostracized for her rather scandalous life (4:17–18). What was most unusual to the woman was that Jesus, a Jewish man, would deign to speak to her, a Samaritan woman (4:9). Not only did Jews have nothing to do with Samaritans, as the text here notes, but as a rule men did not speak to women in public in that society. Thus when Jesus' disciples return, they are surprised to find him talking with a woman (v. 27). Perhaps, then, the woman asks her question in v. 9 not purely out of surprise but for her own amusement—to goad Jesus a little. She probably thinks that he must be very thirsty indeed to condescend to speak to her. But Jesus' answer to the woman is equally provocative. He says to her, in effect, "You should be asking me for a drink" (4:10). He then captures her interest by mentioning "living water," which perpetually quenches thirst and which is in his power to give (4:13–14). This sounds very attractive to the woman, because of the freedom it offers her from the burdensome task of fetching water each day (4:15).

Jesus switches topics. "Go call your husband," he tells her (4:16). The suddenness of the change in subject may be editorial, as some scholars have suggested. That is, John, the author here, returns to the original story that is his source for this episode. But from a perspective of the overall narrative, the change is quite effective. By it, Jesus initiates a movement in the conversation from physical matters to deeper, spiritual ones. The woman has no husband (4:17), because she has been married five times and currently lives with yet another man (4:18). Her failed relationships and present cohabitation call her moral standards into question and would probably make her a pariah in her society. It is no wonder that she now quickly changes the subject. She turns to one of the primary sources of friction between Jews and Samaritans—whether the proper place of worship is Mount Gerizim in Samaria or Jerusalem (4:20). It is a very provocative question, whose answer—almost any answer—could easily offend. To answer, "Jerusalem, of course," with most Jews would offend the woman and drive her away. But to take the Samaritan side by answering "Mount Gerizim" would be disingenuous and offensive to Jesus' disciples and probably John's readers. Jesus' answer, therefore, is brilliant and unexpected (4:21–24). It is not where one worships God that counts but how, that is, with what attitude. When the woman mentions the expected Messiah (4:25), Jesus reveals that he is the Messiah (4:26). At that moment the disciples return (4:27), and the woman goes back to her village to announce her discovery to her neighbors (4:28).

The woman's wisdom is suggested by the way in which she

approaches her fellow townsfolk with the news about the Messiah. She does not simply declare to them her conclusion about who Jesus is. She knows that as a woman whose marriages and current lifestyle are known, the villagers will not listen to her. Instead she raises the question, "He couldn't be the Messiah, could he?" (4:29), thus inviting them to see for themselves. So they flock to Jesus with curious and open minds (4:30), and he describes their approach as fields ripe for harvesting (4:35). Many of them do indeed come to believe in Jesus (4:39–41), and perhaps it is, as they claim, because they see and hear for themselves (4:42). Nevertheless, it was the woman's experience and testimony that first opened the door to them.

This beautiful story portrays Jesus as a person who ignored the social barriers common in his day—barriers based on gender, ethnicity, and even religion. As in Luke, in this story Jesus found that the most receptive person is often the one who is the outcast or pariah. There were many differences between Jesus and the woman, many reasons for him to ignore her. She was a reviled Samaritan, a woman, and a sinner. But none of these things mattered, and in the end he gave her the living water.

The Good Shepherd (10:11–18)

The well-known metaphor of Jesus as the good shepherd comes from John 10. Just as a devoted shepherd risks his life for the sheep under his care, so Jesus lays his life down, he says, for his sheep (10:11, 15). Jesus adds in v. 16 that he has other sheep of different folds that he must bring in also. Then, he says, there will be one shepherd and one flock. The words in this verse allude to the addition of Gentiles to the "flock," the community of the saved. What is particularly remarkable about these statements is the enormous value they place on the formation of a unified community of believers. Christians often think in individual, "vertical" terms: "Jesus died to save me." The perspective of John 10:16 is quite different. The good shepherd came to bring sheep from different folds together into a single flock, and he lays down his life for them all. The verse hints at an idea that Paul will state explicitly—that the reason for Jesus' incarnation was to unite human beings.

That They May All Be One (17:20–23)

On the eve of Jesus' arrest and subsequent crucifixion, the Gospel of John recounts the moving prayer for the disciples in John 17. Jesus asks for protection on their behalf—not from the persecution that will come to them because of their faith (v. 14) but from "the evil one" (v. 15) who will tempt them to apostasy and disloyalty through that persecution. He ends the prayer with a special plea for unity—not only for those who are his followers at the time but for all "those who will believe in me through their word" (v. 20). The model is the unity of Jesus with God, the "Father" (v. 21). In fact, Jesus summarizes the goal of his entire mission to earth as being to effect perfect unity between God, himself, and his followers (v. 23). It is through the perfect unity among the believers that the world will recognize Jesus (v. 23). Again, as hinted in the good shepherd passage, God's act in Christ is described in this passage as a dual process, involving uniting humans to one another and humanity as a whole to God. It is no accident that Jesus' prayer for unity occurs immediately before his trial and death. God's purpose in sending Jesus to the earth and to the cross is unity, both horizontally and vertically. Jesus died to bring people together!

Remaining in
the Fellowship (1 John)

Another striking reference to the importance of the Christian community is found in the letter of 1 John. It is not certain whether the author of this letter was the same John who wrote the Gospel, though the language of the two books is often similar. Like the prologue to the Gospel, 1 John opens by referring to "the beginning" (1:1). First John also speaks of Jesus as the "Word," and the author says he was a witness to the "Word of life" that was with the "Father" and has been revealed to "us," apparently a reference to Jesus' earliest followers (1:2). First John goes on to say that the reason he and the other early disciples ("we") testified about the Word was so that those who hear (specifically his audience for the book in this case) might join in fellowship with those disciples. As in the Gospel, the writer of 1 John suggests that Jesus' coming, "the revelation of the Word," was to bring people together, or, as he puts it, into "fellowship" with each other. The Greek word for fellowship is *koinonia*, and it could also be translated "community." The community of which 1 John speaks includes not only humans but God "the Father and his Son Jesus Christ" (1:3).

The precise situation addressed by the letter of 1 John is uncertain and can only be surmised from the contents of the letter itself. Apparently, though, 1 John addresses a church confronted with a type of early heresy known as Gnosticism (from the Greek word for "knowledge," so called because the Gnostics claimed to possess special, esoteric knowledge about God and Jesus). Much of the language in the book consists of terms and images that were common in Gnostic writings, and several of the book's assertions seem designed to counter Gnostic teaching. For example, the contrast in 1:5–10 between light and darkness seems to draw on Gnostic jargon. The message, however, is against Gnostic thought. God is light, but the Gnostics walk in darkness. They say they "know" God but are liars, because they do not keep God's commands (2:4). The author says that those who truly know God listen to "us" (4:6).

In combating the Gnostic influence, the author of 1 John stresses the importance of "remaining" in the "fellowship"— both are key words in the letter. This is apparently because many of the Gnostics have already left the church, claiming to follow a higher "knowledge": "They went out from us, but were not of us" (2:19). In so doing they have turned their backs on the *koinonia* ("fellowship" or "communion") of the church. Thus, throughout the letter, this John encourages his readers to remain faithful to or abide in what they learned "from the beginning" (2:24). Remaining in the church is the difference between life and death—eternal life (2:25). First John 1:7 explains why this is so: "If we walk in the light as he himself is in the light, we have fellowship with one another, and the blood of Jesus his Son cleanses us from all sin (NRSV)." It is in the *koinonia* of the church that the blood of Christ is at work cleansing the faithful. Thus John can say that no one who abides in him sins (3:6). The effecting of community among human beings is not only a significant part of the reason for Christ's coming and death, it is also within that community that the cleansing blood of Christ is at work. It is truly the salvation community. Only by remaining in the fellowship is there communion with God and cleansing from sin, so that to leave the church is to walk away from salvation.

First John also equates remaining in the church with love. The essence of the Christian message is love (3:11)—a selfless love that even means laying down one's life (3:16). Those who love their brothers and sisters stay in the community and thus in the light (2:10). If the Gnostics really loved their fellow Christians, they would have remained in the church to share the special knowledge they claimed to possess. But those who do not love do not really know God (4:8). Not only is communion with God to be found in the church but God is love (4:8), so to remain in the church is to abide in love and hence to abide in God (2:28).

Conclusion

The theology of the Gospel of John and the letter of 1 John offers a significant challenge to the segregation of churches along racial lines as is commonly practiced in this country. Both books make the point that God's purpose in the incarnation, the Word becoming flesh, was to build community, to establish fellowship among all people and between people and God. The Gospel makes clear that all people are eligible for inclusion in this fellowship. The Samaritans cannot be excluded, because the principal source of division between them and the Jews is removed in the new epoch initiated by Christ. The place of worship is no longer important; it is the proper attitude that counts. Jesus' final prayer for the unity of all his followers, on the eve of his arrest and crucifixion, shows just how significant human unity is—it is the reason Christ died! In 1 John, the writer asserts that salvation can only be found in the community (*koinonia*), because it is there that the cleansing blood of Jesus is at work. Those who leave to form a separate community of what they regard as the superior or elite or "knowledge-able" have in fact turned their backs on the love of God. How much more would this apply to those who exclude others from their communities on the basis of race or refuse to have fellowship with others whom they regard as racially inferior! In the final chapter of this book we will see that Paul puts forward a theological case against segregation that is equally forceful, if not more so.

13

"Many Members, yet One Body"

Unity in Diversity
in the Writings of Paul

Rioting erupted in the black community of the city of Memphis after the assassination of Dr. Martin Luther King Jr. in April 1968. Across town lived a white man also named Luther, who owned a business in one of the areas where rioting was the worst. His store was burned and looted—a total loss. Instead of being bitter, he took it as a call to serve. A leader in his church, he convinced his fellow leaders that they should begin an outreach ministry to black sections of the city. They purchased an old school bus and started picking up children to bring them to Sunday school and church.

The response was overwhelming, and soon they added more buses and more routes. Since one of the routes passed close by a sister congregation, the leaders felt that they should make a courtesy call to a representative of that congregation, seeking approval to evangelize in its neighborhoods. They were surprised by the reaction. "We're happy for you to run your buses over here," they were told, "because the more coloreds you import, the more of your white members are leaving and coming here." Still, the leaders were dedicated to the outreach ministry. They took pride in the conviction that it was a positive response to the racial division of the city and the right thing to do, even at the cost of some white members.

As the number of black faces in Sunday school classes and church increased, however, other problems arose. The new children were unaccustomed to the solemnity of the worship services and were often disruptive. They also lacked training in the Bible, so the Sunday school teachers became frustrated or had to simplify their lessons. Regular members complained that their children's needs were being overlooked. A decade or so later, the leadership decided to designate classes specifically for "outreach" children and to isolate them in their own controlled setting for worship. Following this, visitors and prospective members were assured that the separation of white and black children was not racially motivated but based on different educational and disciplinary needs. Leaders continued to boast about their "outreach ministry," but with the segregation of "outreach" children, interest among both white workers and black children waned. Eventually, the program died out. No further measures at integrating the church were ever attempted.

Despite the progress of the civil rights movement in the 1960s and the following decades, racism is still very much an issue in this country. Racial integration, which has crept into schools, businesses, and other institutions in America, tragically has made little headway in its churches. Fannie Lou Hamer's observation about the Sunday morning church service being the most segregated hour in America is as true today as it was twenty years ago. This chapter will cover another theological mandate for integration, this time from Paul, whose case for it is even stronger than John's.

The Judaizer controversy that Luke describes in the early days of the church did not instantly dissipate with the drafting of the letter from the Jerusalem conference in Acts 15. When Paul went on from Antioch to spread the gospel among the Gentiles in other places, he frequently had to combat the same Judaizing efforts. There was nothing wrong with keeping Jewish ritual practices; many Jewish Christians continued to do just that. And Jewish Christians had also accepted non-Jews into the church, at least theoretically. The question, again, was whether Gentiles were to be accepted as they were or whether they should be required to observe Jewish customs, particularly circumcision. At several points in his writings Paul deals with the issue of balancing the unity that should exist in the church with the diversity that individual Christians bring as people of different racial, cultural, and social backgrounds.

All Israel Will Be Saved:
Romans 9—11

Paul's letter to the Romans is regarded by many New Testament scholars as the clearest, most extensive exposition of his theology. In chapters 9—11 he discusses the relationship between Jews and Gentiles. He begins (9:1–10:3) with God's election of Israel and his own devotion to his people. His great desire is for their salvation (10:1), and he says he could wish to be damned for their sake (9:3). But despite the advantages the Jews had as the chosen people, things have changed in Christ. He is the end (in the sense of "fulfillment" or "objective") of the law, so that righteousness is now available to all who believe in him (10:4). As a result, there is no longer any distinction in God's eyes between Jews and Gentiles (10:12), but "everyone who calls on the name of the Lord will be saved" (10:13; cf. Joel 2:32). Paul goes on to argue that this does not mean that God has rejected the chosen people, Israel (11:1–10), but that their disobedience has allowed the inclusion of the Gentiles (11:11–16). He uses the analogy of a tree (11:17–24): Israel is that tree. Some of its branches were broken off, but this allowed others (the Gentiles) to be grafted on. Eventually, however, "all Israel will be saved" (11:26). This is a difficult passage, and scholars debate whether Paul is referring to ethnic Israel (i.e., Jews) or spiritual Israel (i.e., the entire salvation community, regardless of ethnicity). Paul may well have harbored a hope that the Jews as a whole would one day accept Christ. But whatever his understanding in that regard, his point that God now accepts all people is what is important for us.

Neither Jew nor Greek:
The Book of Galatians

Paul's letter to the Galatians, more than any other, recalls his continuing struggles with the Judaizers. He begins the letter by pronouncing a curse on anyone, even an angel from heaven, who would preach to the Galation churches a different gospel from that which they heard at the beginning (1:7–9). He recounts his own conversion and says that he was specially chosen by God to carry the name of Jesus to the Gentiles (1:13–17). His point is that he received the gospel that he preaches directly from Jesus and not from any human agent (1:11–12). The "different gospel" to which he refers and against which he warns the Galatians apparently has to do with the Judaizer controversy, because he launches in chapter 2 into a discussion of the issue of circumcision. Again, he affirms that his mission is to the Gentiles (the "uncircumcised," 2:7). Even Peter and Barnabas, he says, were deceived by the Judaizers' insincerity (2:11–14). He goes on to argue that circumcision and uncircumcision are insignificant for salvation, since a person is justified before God not by works of the law, but by faith (2:15–21), and this faith is accessible to all people, Jews and Gentiles. In his third chapter Paul cites Abraham himself as an example of this principle. Abraham was declared righteous, not by virtue of his ethnic background or of his following the law, but because of his faith (3:6–14). The law was important as a "disciplinarian" to convey people to Christ (3:19–22). But now faith has come and the law is not necessary anymore (3:25). Access to God is no longer through ethnic identity or adherence to the law, but rather through faith in Jesus Christ (3:26). Thus, *anyone* who has been baptized into Christ has put on Christ. Ethnic distinctions are insignificant as far as God is concerned.

There is neither Jew nor Greek, there is neither slave nor free, there is neither male nor female; for you are all one in Christ Jesus. (Gal. 3:28, RSV)

One Body with Many Parts
(1 Cor. 12:12–30)

When Paul says that the differences of race or ethnicity, gender, and social status no longer exist in Christ, he does not mean that God's intention is to obliterate the differences between people that make each person a unique individual. Christians obviously retain their separate identities as men and women and as members of different cultures, races, social groups, and socioeconomic levels. Paul is expressing a paradox: in the church there is diversity in unity. Moreover, this diversity is not merely a matter of necessity. It is a gift from God. It is wholesome and beneficial. Part of the church's strength lies in the diversity of its members, as Paul makes clear in his analogy of the body in 1 Corinthians 12.

In the Corinthian church there were severe divisions over various matters, including "preacher loyalties" (1:11–17) and social status (chap. 11). There were even lawsuits between Christians (6:1–8). Paul wrote to this badly divided church in order to reunite them:

> I appeal to you, brethren, by the name of our Lord Jesus Christ, that all of you agree and that there be no dissensions among you, but that you be united in the same mind and the same judgment. (1 Cor. 1:10, RSV)

As one of the preachers to whom loyalty was being claimed, Paul wrote, "Is Christ divided? Was Paul crucified for you? Or were you baptized in the name of Paul?" (1:13, RSV). Christ died to bring people together, not to cause separation into warring factions.

In 1 Corinthians 12—14 Paul turns to another source of division in the Corinthian church—the different spiritual gifts exercised by various members. He uses the image of the body to illustrate the principle of diversity in unity. The church is the body of Christ. Like a human body, it is one, a single unit, yet with many members (12:12). As each individual body has a spirit, so the members of Christ's body share the divine Spirit (12:13). Yet, the members of this body are diverse. They come from different races, cultures, social levels, and so on (12:13). They also have different functions in the body of the church, according to their various gifts and abilities. This diversity is according to the plan and purpose of God (v. 18), who is the distributor of the gifts of the members (vv. 28–30).

Paul paints a ludicrous image of the body. It would be ridiculous for a foot to secede from the body because it wants to be a hand (v. 15) or for an ear to leave the body because it cannot be an eye (v. 16). It is equally ludicrous for a member of Christ's body to pout out of envy of another member's talents and function in the church. Yet this is apparently what some of the Corinthian Christians were doing. The church needs the diversity of its members, with their different functions and talents. The gifts that allow for that diversity are God-given.

Another set of ludicrous images described here by Paul is conceived of as a result of one member's conceit at its own function and abilities. This image was also inspired by a problem in the Corinthian church, where some gifts were being valued more than others and those who possessed them were being privileged above other members. Again, it is ridiculous to imagine an eye regarding the ear as useless or the hand believing the foot to be unnecessary (v. 21). In both sets of ludicrous examples Paul's point is plain. Not only does the body as a whole need the diversity of its members but the members need one another's diversity of functions. The beauty of the body is in its various members. Each member performs its individual function, but all are directed toward a common goal. All members work together for the good of the whole. So it should be in the church as well. Christians should prize their different gifts and abilities. Without them the church would be boring and unable to accomplish very much.

The absurdity of the Corinthians' petty squabbling over gifts, their jealousies and conceits, is illustrated by the image of the body as a single organ (vv. 17–19). A body that had only eyes for members could do nothing but see (v. 17a). A six-foot ear could not see, smell, walk, or talk (v. 17b); it could only hear. The body needs its diversity, and so does the church. Each member and that member's function are important to the body and to the church. God has designed the church in this way. Envy and conceit have no place in the body of Christ. If everyone were the same, there would be no body (v. 19).

Another point drawn by Paul from this analogy of the body has to do with the honor ascribed to the various members (vv. 22–25). Here again there is a paradox. Those body parts that seem weakest and receive the least recognition are often among the most important for the functioning of the body. So it is in the body of Christ. Paul says that God has arranged the church so that those members who receive the most honor are actually the inferior ones, and those who are most important are least honored. Paul is especially addressing the situation in the Corinthian church with regard to those who had the gift of speaking in tongues. Although it is one of the most obvious and envied gifts, Paul says that it is among the least important for the church. Thus, those who speak in tongues should not be conceited. Other, less noticeable gifts are actually more necessary for the body. Perhaps the same point could be applied to the church today as well. Those Christians who receive the least honor and recognition may actually be the ones who are most essential to the church.

God's objective in arranging the body is intimate sympathy among the members in which the members experience all things equally together (v. 26). One may expand on this aspect of the analogy by raising ludicrous questions, as Paul himself did earlier. If the hand is injured, does the hand alone suffer? Is not the entire body affected? If one wins a race, do the feet alone receive a prize? Is not the entire body honored? What Paul describes here is true *koinonia*, "fellowship" or "community." All members share the honor or suffering that comes to any individual member. All members work for the good of the body, not for themselves. This unselfishness is best described as love. Indeed, *koinonia* and *agape* are intimately related and very significant for the development of the body of Christ. It is no accident that the great passage on love, 1 Corinthians 13, immediately follows Paul's use of the body imagery in 1 Corinthians 12:12–30. Paul's description of love is not an abstract definition, but is tailor-made for the situation of the Corinthian church. Love is the "greatest gift" (12:31; 13:13). It is the opposite of envy and conceit, which Paul ridicules and combats by means of the body analogy (13:4–7). Without love, the gifts over which the Corinthians are fighting are useless (13:1–3), and unlike those gifts love never ends (13:8–13). Love describes the active attitude that Christians must exercise toward one another if they are to maintain the unity of the body of Christ and carry out their various functions within his body.

Paul enlarges on the analogy of the body in Romans 12:4–8. Here he states that Christians are members of one another in the body of Christ. He lists some of the functions and gifts that distinguish Christians. These include prophecy, service, teaching, exhortation, contributing, and giving aid. Paul encourages his readers to use their gifts for the good of the body. It is clear that the list in these verses is not intended to be a complete set of all possible gifts and functions of Christians. However, every Christian surely possesses at least one of the gifts in this list in some measure. Every member has a gift and function in the body of Christ (v. 6); every Christian is significant for the church. Hence, Paul admonishes his readers not to think more of themselves than they ought (v. 3). Again, as in 1 Corinthians 12—13, it is no accident that after discussing the diversity of gifts in the body of Christ (Rom. 12:4–8), Paul admonishes the Romans to love (12:9–10). He tells them to love one another genuinely and to work to give one another the greater honor (v. 9). Unselfish love is essential if the diverse members are to maintain their unity.

In Ephesians 4:11 there is another partial list of the gifts given by God to different parts of the body of Christ. This list includes apostles, prophets, evangelists, pastors, and teachers (or teaching pastors). These gifts specifically are mentioned because the letter addresses Christians who are facing false doctrine. Its particular concern is that the readers be prepared to face those who would lead them astray, so it concentrates on those who have gifts relating to teaching. This is not to say that these are the only gifts and ministries or even necessarily the most important ones. The function of the people with these gifts is "to equip the saints for the work of ministry" (v. 12). Their purpose is to keep the church from being "tossed to and fro and blown about by every wind of doctrine, by people's trickery by their craftiness in deceitful scheming" (v. 14, NRSV). Those who are thus led astray are immature children (v. 14). The opposite condition is that of mature adulthood (v. 13). The church, as the body of Christ, is to grow and develop into maturity just as the physical body grows. Correct teaching will help the body to grow, but the element that really holds the body together is love. Thus, the body grows when its members speak the truth in love (v. 15). It is in love that the body upbuilds itself (v. 16). Love is the true sign of spiritual maturity. One is again reminded of 1 Corinthians 13:11, where Paul contrasts childish thinking and actions with the maturity of love.

Breaking Down Barriers
(Eph. 2:11–22)

One of the most amazing passages in the writings attributed to Paul, indeed in all of the New Testament, is this one from Ephesians 2. Most New Testament scholars doubt that Paul actually wrote Ephesians, but see it instead as the work of a disciple close to Paul. It is also uncertain whether the letter was originally destined specifically for the Ephesians. The initial greeting is general and does not mention any names. The phrase "in Ephesus" in 1:1 is textually dubious and may not have been in the original letter. Thus the book may actually have been a general letter or homily that circulated among churches in Asia Minor. But whatever its origin, it develops Paul's theology and attaches enormous significance to human fellowship in the work of Christ and in the church. No passage testifies more forcefully to God's hatred of racism than Ephesians 2, and because of this it is an appropriate text with which to close our study.

Earlier in this chapter, the writer explores the grace given to Christians through faith in Christ. All people, he says, regardless of race, were dead in sin (2:1–3). But God's love, again for all people, brings life, hope, and salvation (2:4–7):

> But God, who is rich in mercy, through his great love with which he loved us even while we were dead in sins, made us alive together with Christ. (Eph. 2:4–5)

Salvation, therefore, is not a matter of race or nationality or of adherence to a code of laws or rules. Rather, it is a matter of God's grace activated through faith.

> For by grace you have been saved through faith, and this not of yourselves; it is God's gift. (Eph. 2:8)

The second half of the chapter describes the effects of God's grace on relationships between humans in the church. The Gentiles, say verses 11–13, were once "far away" from the salvation community. They were aliens and foreigners to Israel, not included in God's covenant with the chosen people and therefore without hope. But in Christ they have been brought "near." Christ has broken down the "dividing wall of hostility" that kept the Gentiles out (2:14). As a result, the Gentiles can now be admitted to the salvation community as full members. The unity between Jew and Gentile is effected in Christ's flesh—by his coming in the flesh, as a human, and in his body, the church.

The word used to describe the working of God's grace is "peace." Jesus himself is "our peace" (v. 14) because he broke down the wall that separated Jews and Gentiles. In verse 15, the writer defines that wall as the law—the "commandments and ordinances" that distinguished Jews from Gentiles. In Christ, he says, that wall is removed. It is not necessary for either group to keep the law, because salvation is through God's grace in Christ. Paul's use of "peace" here is pregnant with meaning. Jews and Gentiles are both reconciled and united. The description of

Jesus' work as peacemaker here seems to play on different concepts of peace. One concept is the mere cessation of conflict as in v. 14, where the dividing wall of hostility is removed. This is the meaning of the Greek word for peace, *eirene*. The other concept is the Hebrew notion of *shalom*—harmony and completeness. The Semitic concept is found particularly in v. 15, where Christ creates a new individual. In Christ, God has not only removed the cause of hostility between Jews and Gentiles (the Greek meaning of "peace"), but has also brought about complete unity and tranquillity (*shalom*). Christ has done this by creating in himself one new person in place of the two hostile individuals (v. 15). Finally, Jesus effects peace in two directions at once—horizontally and vertically. He reconciles humans to one another and then the new humanity to God. Christ has presented the newly created, unified humanity to God for reconciliation through the cross (v. 16). Thus, in Christ both Jews and Gentiles are at peace with God (v. 17) and have access to God through the Spirit. In verses 17–21, the metaphor changes. In Christ, Gentiles are made part of the "house of Israel" (v. 19). The early Christian leaders are the foundation, and Jesus himself is the cornerstone of the structure (v. 20). It is a living, spiritual building, a temple, in which both Jewish and Gentile elements thrive and grow jointly (vv. 21–22).

What is most striking about this passage is the significance it ascribes to human relationships as a purpose for Christ's coming and death. The writer says that one of the main reasons for the coming of Christ was to bring people together. The passage describes reconciliation with God and reconciliation between people as results of the same act of Christ. They are both part of one package! Moreover, as it is stated here, the horizontal reconciliation comes first. Christ unites Jews and Gentiles in order to present the one new person to God for reconciliation. The text clearly stresses the importance of harmony among Christians. The significance that it attaches to this horizontal reconciliation as a major purpose for the death of Jesus is astounding, given the fact that Christians have tended to overlook this dimension and to think of reconciliation as occurring only vertically, between God and people.

Summary and Conclusions

While differences of culture and especially race have been the focus of our study, they are not the only potential barriers to harmony among humans. The writings attributed to Paul deal with other "dividing walls of hostility" brought about through differences of gender and social status. Galatians 3:28 is worth quoting again:

> There is neither Jew nor Greek, there is neither slave nor free, there is neither male nor female; for you are all one in Christ Jesus. (RSV)

First Corinthians 12:13 introduces the analogy of the church as body this way:

> For in one Spirit we all were baptized into one body, Jews or Greeks, slaves or free, and all were given to drink of one Spirit.

In Colossians 3:11 Paul speaks of the new life in Christ that is available to all people regardless of ethnic and social differences:

> There is neither Greek nor Jew, circumcised or uncircumcised, barbarian [a word for non-Greek speakers], Scythian [the epitome of pagans, according to Romans], slave, or free, but Christ is all in all.

In the letter to Philemon, Paul even mediates between a runaway slave and his master. Their relationship has changed because Onesimus is "no longer a slave but more than a slave, a beloved brother" (v. 16). The point throughout the Pauline material is that the differences that separate people from one another and lead to prejudice and discrimination do not matter in God's eyes. The capstone to this argument is Ephesians 2, which says that Christ came to unite people of all kinds.

Unity with diversity is as important for the church today as it was for the New Testament church. The temptation for Christians of all eras is to require conformity. Perhaps it is human nature for individuals to be uncomfortable with people different from themselves. Hence, the tendency, since the Judaizers, has been for Christians to form congregations made up of homogeneous members—people of the same race and social level, who dress alike, think alike, even look alike. Thus, it is no accident that churches in the United States have basically formed along racial lines. But the New Testament describes Christians in terms of unity, not uniformity. There is no doctrine of segregation in the New Testament. Its credo is not "separate but equal"; it is "different but united." Christians of all races and ethnicities (not to mention social levels and genders) are equal in God's eyes. But this does not mean they are the same. The church's health and strength lie in the diversity of its members. Maybe the shape of U.S. churches would be different if the Christians understood the premium that the Bible as a whole places on human harmony and that the New Testament places on the diversity of individual members within the unity of Christ's body.

Notes

1. Henry Hampton and Steve Fayer, with Sarah Flynn,

Voices of Freedom: An Oral History of the Civil Rights Movement from the 1950s Through the 1980s (New York: Bantam Books, 1990). The book is a publication of the interviews on which the acclaimed PBS series *Eyes on the Prize* is based.

2. "Yahweh" is God's name in the Old Testament. Some English translations render it as "Jehovah" or "LORD" (in all capitals).

3. "Sarai" (meaning unclear) is also changed to Sarah, meaning "princess."

4. Most English translations of 1 Samuel 15:32 have Agag the Amalekite king come cheerfully saying, "Surely the bitterness of death is past," as though he has received a reprieve from Saul. But there is a textual problem in this verse, and a better reading is that Agag is brought bound in chains (or possibly "trembling") and says, "Is death as bitter as this?" See the NRSV translation. In other words, Agag was not reprieved or well treated by Saul at all and was certainly not cheerful. With his people annihilated, he expected and perhaps longed for death himself.

5. The NRSV unfortunately obscures the nature of the book's audience by translating "son" as "child."

6. The Hebrew word *massa'* in both Prov. 30:1 and 31:1 can also mean "oracle." Thus, 31:1 can be translated, "The words of Lemuel, a king, an oracle which his mother taught him." The main problem with this interpretation is that Proverbs 31 does not contain an oracle. The NRSV's translation, "The words of King Lemuel . . ." is simply incorrect. In 30:1, the word *massa'* is probably an addition influenced by its occurrence in 31:1. It is repetitive in a way because another word meaning "oracle"

occurs immediately after it. It is also intrusive and must be changed somehow in order to make sense of it. Thus, while the Hebrew text has "the oracle," the NRSV changes it to read "an oracle," and the RSV adds either a preposition or a suffix to get the translation "of Massa." It remains clear that chapter 31 is ascribed to a non-Israelite, since no king of Israel or Judah was named Lemuel. It is less certain that Agur of 30:1 was non-Israelite.

7. Most scholars see Isaiah 56—66 as an even later addition to the book, and call it "Third Isaiah."

8. Hans Walter Wolff, *Joel and Amos,* Hermeneia Commentary (Philadelphia: Fortress Press, 1977), 347.

9. "Sick and Tired of Being Sick and Tired," by Fannie Lou Hamer. Originally published in the journal *Katallagete—Be Reconciled,* the quotation here is from a 1972 reprinted version in *The Future and the Hope: Essays of Southern Churchmen,* ed. Will D. Campbell and James Y. Holloway (Grand Rapids: Wm. B. Eerdmans Publishing Co.), 162–64. Reprinted by permission of Will D. Campbell.

10. The final phrase, "and with all your mind," is not in Deut. 6:5 but was either added by Luke or was in the version of Deuteronomy that he had.

11. The additional dialogue of v. 37 ("Philip said, 'If you believe with all your heart you may.' And he replied, 'I believe Jesus Christ to be the son of God'") fits the moment well but is not in the best ancient manuscripts of the book of Acts.

12. I owe this observation to Cain Hope Felder, "Race, Racism, and the Biblical Narratives," in *Stony the Road We Trod: African American Biblical Interpretation,* ed. Cain Hope Felder (Minneapolis: Fortress Press, 1991), 143.

13. Careful readers will notice that James's citation differs from Amos 9:11–12 in their English versions. This is partly because James apparently mixes in elements of other passages (especially Isa. 45:21) and partly because he cites a different version of Amos to begin with. The version he cites supports his argument about the Gentiles, and this is the important point.

For Further Study

Chapter 1:
"In the Image of God"

McKenzie, Steven L. "Cush" and "Ham/Canaan, Cursing of." In *The Oxford Companion to the Bible,* edited by Bruce M. Metzger and Michael D. Coogan, 145, 268. New York: Oxford University Press, 1993.

Rad, Gerhard von. *Genesis: A Commentary.* Rev. ed. Philadelphia: Westminster Press, 1972.

Speiser, E. A. *Genesis.* Anchor Bible. Garden City, N.Y.: Doubleday & Co., 1964.

Van Seters, John. *Prologue to History: The Yahwist as Historian in Genesis.* Louisville, Ky.: Westminster/John Knox Press, 1992.

Westermann, Claus. *Genesis: A Practical Commentary.* Translated by David E. Green. Grand Rapids: Wm. B. Eerdmans Publishing Co., 1987.

Chapter 2:
"All the Families of the Earth"

Pritchard, James B., ed. *Ancient Near Eastern Texts Relating to the Old Testament,* 3d ed., with Supplement. Princeton, N.J.: Princeton University Press, 1969.

Van Seters, John. *Abraham in History and Tradition.* New Haven, Conn.: Yale University Press, 1975.

Chapter 3:
"You Must Utterly Destroy Them"

Craigie, Peter C. *The Problem of War in the Old Testament*. Grand Rapids: Wm. B. Eerdmans Publishing Co., 1978.

Dearman, Andrew, ed. *Studies in the Mesha Inscription and Moab*. Atlanta: Scholars Press, 1989.

Hobbs, T. R. *A Time for War: A Study of Warfare in the Old Testament*. Wilmington, Del.: Michael Glazier, 1989.

Kang, Sa-Moon. *Divine War in the Old Testament and the Ancient Near East*. BZAW 177. Berlin: Walter de Gruyter, 1989.

Lind, Millard C. *Yahweh Is a Warrior: The Theology of Warfare in Ancient Israel*. Scottdale, Pa.: Herald Press, 1980.

Rad, Gerhard von. *Holy War in Ancient Israel*. Translated by M. J. Dawn. Grand Rapids: Wm. B. Eerdmans Publishing Co., 1991.

Stern, Philip D. *The Biblical* Herem: *A Window on Israel's Religous Experience*. Brown Judaic Studies 211. Atlanta: Scholars Press, 1991.

Chapter 4:
"A Mixed Crowd"

The Anchor Bible Dictionary. Edited by David Noel Freedman, et al. New York: Doubleday & Co., 1992. The following articles may be of interest:

David W. Baker, "Cushan," I:1219–20

Rita J. Burns, "Zipporah," VI:1105

Leonard J. Greenspoon, "Rahab (PERSON)," V:611–12

Niels Peter Lemche, "Hebrew," III:95

George E. Mendenhall, "Midian," IV:815–18

Van Seters, John. *The Life of Moses: The Yahwist as Historian in Exodus–Numbers*. Louisville, Ky.: Westminster John Knox Press, 1994.

Chapter 5:
"Your People Will Be My People"

Campbell, Edward F. *Ruth.* Anchor Bible. Garden City, N.Y.: Doubleday & Co., 1975.

Fewell, Danna Nolan, and David Miller Gunn. *Compromising Redemption: Relating Characters in the Book of Ruth.* Louisville, Ky.: Westminster/John Knox Press, 1990.

Gow, Murray D. *The Book of Ruth: Its Structure, Theme, and Purpose.* Leicester, England: Apollos, 1992.

Hubbard, Robert L., Jr. *The Book of Ruth.* New International Commentary. Grand Rapids: Wm. B. Eerdmans Publishing Co., 1988.

Sasson, Jack M. *Ruth: A New Translation with a Philological Commentary and a Formalist-Folklorist Interpretation.* 2d ed. Sheffield: Journal for the Study of the Old Testament, 1989.

Trible, Phyllis. "Ruth, Book of." In *The Anchor Bible Dictionary.* Vol. 5, 842–47. New York: Doubleday & Co., 1992.

Chapter 6:
"You Shall Have No Part with Us"

Blenkinsopp, Joseph. *Ezra-Nehemiah: A Commentary.* Old Testament Library. Philadelphia: Westminster Press, 1988.

Glazier-McDonald, Beth. *Malachi: The Divine Messenger.* SBL Dissertation Series 98. Atlanta: Scholars Press, 1987.

Japhet, Sara. *I & II Chronicles: A Commentary.* Old Testament Library. Louisville, Ky.: Westminster/John Knox Press, 1993.

Klein, Ralph W. "Ezra–Nehemiah, Books of." In *The Anchor Bible Dictionary.* Vol. 2, 731–42. New York: Doubleday & Co., 1992.

McKenzie, Steven L., and Howard N. Wallace. "Covenant Themes in Malachi," *Catholic Biblical Quarterly* 45 (1983): 549–63.

Williamson, H.G.M. *Ezra, Nehemiah.* Word Biblical Commentary. Waco, Tex.: Word, 1985.

———. *Israel in the Books of Chronicles.* Cambridge: Cambridge University Press, 1977.

Chapter 7:
"The Ear That Hears and the Eye That Sees"

Crenshaw, James L. *Urgent Advice and Probing Questions: Collected Writings on Old Testament Wisdom.* Macon, Ga.: Mercer University Press, 1995.

Murphy, Roland E. *The Tree of Life: An Exploration of Biblical Wisdom Literature.* Anchor Bible Reference Library. New York: Doubleday & Co., 1990.

———. "Wisdom in the OT." In *The Anchor Bible Dictionary.* VI:920–31. New York: Doubleday & Co., 1992.

Chapter 8:
"I Knew That You Are a Merciful God"

LaCocque, André, and Pierre-Emmanuel LaCocque, *Jonah: A Psycho-Religious Approach to the Prophet.* Columbia, S.C.: University of South Carolina Press, 1990.

Limburg, James. *Jonah: A Commentary.* Louisville, Ky.: Westminster/John Knox Press, 1993.

Sasson, Jack M. *Jonah.* Anchor Bible. New York: Doubleday & Co., 1990.

Trible, Phyllis. *Rhetorical Criticism: Context, Method, and the Book of Jonah.* Minneapolis: Fortress, 1994.

Wolff, Hans Walter. *Obadiah and Jonah: A Commentary.* Translated by M. Kohl. Minneapolis: Augsburg, 1986.

Chapter 9:
"Him Shall the Nations Seek"

Holladay, William L. *Jeremiah.* Vol. 1. Hermeneia Commentary. Philadelphia: Fortress Press, 1986.

Kaiser, Otto. *Isaiah 1—12: A Commentary.* 2d ed. Translated by J. Bowden. Philadelphia: Westminster Press, 1983.

Paul, Shalom M. *Amos.* Hermeneia Commentary. Minneapolis: Fortress Press, 1991.

Seitz, Christopher. *Isaiah 1—39.* Louisville, Ky.: Westminster/John Knox Press, 1993.

Ward, James M. *Amos & Isaiah: Prophets of the Word of God.* Nashville: Abingdon Press, 1969.

Chapter 10:
"The Spirit of the Lord Is upon Me"

Fitzmyer, Joseph A. *The Gospel according to Luke.* 2 vols., Anchor Bible. Garden City, N.Y.: Doubleday & Co., 1981, 1985.

Jervell, Jacob. *Luke and the People of God: A New Look at Luke–Acts.* Minneapolis: Augsburg, 1972.

Sanders, Jack T. *The Jews in Luke–Acts.* Philadelphia: Fortress Press, 1987.

Wilson, Stephen G. *The Gentiles and the Gentile Mission in Luke–Acts.* Cambridge: Cambridge University Press, 1973.

Chapter 11:
"Nothing Common or Unclean"

Barrett, C. K. *The Acts of the Apostles.* Vol. 1. The International Critical Commentary. Edinburgh: T. & T. Clark, 1994.

Conzelmann, Hans. *Acts of the Apostles.* Hermeneia Commentary. Philadelphia: Fortress Press, 1987.

Haenchen, Ernst. *The Acts of the Apostles: A Commentary.* Philadelphia: Westminster Press, 1971.

Williams, David J. *Acts.* New International Biblical Commentary. Peabody, Mass.: Hendrickson, 1985.

Chapter 12:
"That They May All Be One"

Barrett, C. K. *The Gospel according to St. John.* 2d ed. London: SPCK, 1978.

Brown, Raymond E. *The Gospel according to John.* 2 vols. Anchor Bible. Garden City, N.Y.: Doubleday & Co., 1966, 1970.

Bultmann, Rudolf. *The Gospel of John: A Commentary.* Translated by G. R. Beasley-Murray. Oxford: Basil Blackwell, 1971.

———. *The Johannine Epistles.* Hermeneia Commentary. Philadelphia: Fortress Press, 1973.

McKenzie, Steven L. "The Church in 1 John." *Restoration Quarterly* 19 (1976): 211–16.

Morris, Leon. *The Gospel according to St. John.* New International Commentary. Grand Rapids: Wm. B. Eerdmans Publishing Co., 1971.

Chapter 13:
"Many Members, yet One Body"

Barrett, C.K. *Essays on Paul.* Philadelphia: Westminster Press, 1982.

Fitzmyer, Joseph A. *Paul and His Theology: A Brief Sketch.* 2d ed. Englewood Cliffs, N.J.: Prentice-Hall, 1989.

Kaylor, R. David. *Paul's Covenant Community: Jew & Gentile in Romans.* Atlanta: John Knox Press, 1988.

Keck, Leander E. *Paul and His Letters.* Proclamation Commentaries. 2d ed. Philadelphia: Fortress Press, 1988.

Robinson, John A. T. *The Body: A Study in Pauline Theology.* Philadelphia: Westminster Press, 1952.

Martin, Ralph P. *Ephesians, Colossians, and Philemon.* Interpretation. Atlanta: John Knox Press, 1991.